HARDY

TESS OF THE D'URBERVILLES

NOTES

COLES EDITORIAL BOARD

A NOTE TO THE READER

These Notes present a clear discussion of the action and thought of the work under consideration and a concise interpretation of its artistic merits and its significance.

They are intended as a supplementary aid to the serious student. They serve to free the student from interminable and distracting note-taking in class so that he may listen intelligently to what the instructor is saying, or to the class discussion, making selective notes on these, secure in the knowledge that he has the basic understanding. They are also helpful in preparing for an examination, saving not merely the burden but the confusion of trying to re-read the full text under pressure, and disentangling from a mass of — often illegible — notes that which is of central importance.

THE NOTES ARE NOT A SUBSTITUTE FOR THE TEXT ITSELF OR FOR THE CLASSROOM DISCUSSION OF THE TEXT, AND THE STUDENT WHO SO ATTEMPTS TO USE THEM IS DENYING HIMSELF THE VERY EDUCATION THAT HE IS PRESUMABLY GIVING HIS MOST VITAL YEARS TO ACHIEVE.

The critical evaluations have been prepared by experts with special knowledge of the individual texts who have usually had some years' experience in teaching the works. They are, however, not incontrovertible. No literary judgment is. Of any great work of literature there are many interpretations, and even conflicting views have value for the student (and the teacher), since the aim is not for the student to accept unquestioningly any one interpretation but to make his own.

ISBN 0-7740-3380-0

©COPYRIGHT 1985 AND PUBLISHED BY
COLES PUBLISHING COMPANY LIMITED
TORONTO — CANADA
PRINTED IN CANADA

CONTENTS

Thomas Hardy: Life and Works

Thomas Hardy (June 2, 1840 - January 11, 1928), novelist and poet, was born close to the Egdon Heath which he made immortal — in Dorset, near Dorchester. He was the oldest child of a prosperous stonemason or builder, a strong handsome man of marked musical talent. His mother came of a long line of yeoman farmers, and had inherited bookish tastes from her own mother.

When the child was born, he was thought to be dead, and was rescued only by the keen perception of a nurse. Until he was six his parents did not expect him to live, and because of his delicacy his mother became his first teacher. He lived to be over eighty-seven, in full possession of his powers and faculties to the last!

Hardy was precocious, and could read before he could talk plainly. He was not sent to school until he was eight. In all he attended four schools from 1848 to 1856, the last the Dorchester Grammar School, founded by one of his own ancestors, and of which he himself was governor from 1909 to 1926. He also studied French at home with a private teacher, and later in London took a few French courses at King's College.

This was the extent of his formal education. At sixteen he was apprenticed to a local ecclesiastical architect, with whom his father had long done business. This man was something of a classical scholar, easy-going and lenient, and he allowed his young apprentice to spend more time in studying Greek than in studying architecture. Perhaps for this reason, Hardy's father sent him in 1862 to study with the eminent architect Sir Arthur Bloomfield. Here again, however, he seems to have had plenty of time for lecturing his fellow students on poetry! It is true that he won a prize in 1863 in a national competition for essays on the application of colored bricks and terra cotta to modern architecture — but the award explicitly says that he is to receive the medal, but not the £10 also offered, since his essay, though splendidly written, does not go very deeply or expertly into the subject.

Hardy nevertheless stayed with Bloomfield until 1867, and afterwards for six years was a practising architect. The chief achievement of his profession was the winning of a wife. In 1870 he went to Cornwall to restore a church, and in 1874 he married the vicar's sister-in-law, Emma Lavinia Gifford.

Meanwhile, he was persistently writing poetry, which was his first literary love and his last. No one would have his poems, and not one of them was published until 1898, when his career as a novelist was over. Actually, his first published work was an anonymous humorous sketch in *Chamber's Journal* which he wrote for the amusement of his associates in Bloomfield's office.

In 1867 he had already written his first novel, *The Poor Man and the*

1

Lady. George Meredith, who was then reader for Chapman and Hall, rejected it on the ground that it "had not enough plot;" and Hardy, whose opinion of his own fiction was always absurdly critical, promptly destroyed the manuscript — perhaps a real loss to English literature. Certainly the next novel, and his first to be published, *Desperate Remedies*, was quite inferior to the one he had burnt, for he took Meredith's advice so seriously that he crowded it with a melodramatic and artificial plot. It too was anonymous, and he had advanced £75 (out of £123 he had in the world) towards its publication, of which only £60 was returned. The only attention it received was a scathing review or two. It is no wonder that, against the wishes of his fiancée, he decided that writing was not his forte and that he must henceforth devote himself strictly to architecture.

Nevertheless he could not keep his itching pen quiet very long. The very next year *Under the Greenwood Tree* appeared, and this time, though he did not make much profit, there was no loss. *A Pair of Blue Eyes* (reminiscent of his courtship days in Cornwall) followed, and Hardy was at last convinced that authorship would enable him to marry and support a wife as well as or better than architecture would do. He became sure of it in 1874, for *Far From the Madding Crowd*, commissioned first as a serial by *Cornhill's Magazine*, was his first great financial and literary success. (Much to Hardy's annoyance, one reviewer guessed the book to be by George Eliot under a new pseudonym!)

On the strength of it the young couple were married and settled down on the outskirts of London. For the next nine years, except for a trip to Holland and Germany, they lived and Hardy worked in various London suburbs. During this time, in 1880, he was bedridden for six months with an alarming series of internal hemorrhages. It is significant of the future that at this very moment when his life hung in the balance, and he was dictating in desperate haste in order to leave some income to his wife should he die, he wrote in his diary that he wanted more and more to devote himself entirely to poetry. This persistent urge throws light on his decision in 1896.

In 1883 the Hardys, for reasons concerning his health, moved to Dorchester. Two years later — probably his last architectural effort — they built their famous house which they called Max Gate. Thereafter most of the year was spent at Max Gate, with a few months in London and occasional tours on the Continent. Hardy frequently regretted the move, but there is no doubt that it helped to prolong his life and efficiency.

The succession of annual or biennial novels, almost every one a masterpiece of its kind, culminated in 1891, in *Tess of the d'Urbervilles*. Hardy had realized that this was strong meat for the conventional tastes of that stodgy era; he had had to mutilate the story badly for magazine publication, before he could restore the shattered limbs for its appearance in book form. The storm of abuse, aimed equally at the "infidelity" and "obscenity" of that mighty tragedy, he took calmly and with humor. It was nothing, however, to the cyclone which burst over his head with the publication of *Jude the Obscure* in 1896. This too had been emasculated for the magazines and then restored — the American serial version made the children of Jude and Sue into Jude's little brothers and sisters, to spare the delicacy of the reader! There had been no such shrieks of horror over a book since Swinburne's *Poems and Ballads* had appeared thirty years before. This powerful, tender study of the frustration of an aspiring soul, alive with indignation at injustice and somberly pitiful, this magnificent psychological analysis, was denounced as mere pornography: the favorite nickname of the critics for the book was "Jude the Obscene." Hardy received a flood of defamatory letters — one reader in Australia sent him the ashes to which she had reduced his "filthy" novel!

It is customary to say that it was because of this reception of his two greatest novels that Hardy announced in 1896 that he would never write fiction again, and kept his word. (*The Well Beloved* was issued as a book in 1897, but had appeared as a serial in 1892.) This is a falsification of a complex situation. Thomas Hardy was hardly to be "snuffed out by an article." Disgusted and depressed by the stupidity of his fellow beings he undoubtedly was. But it has been seen how his heart clung to poetry; he never valued his novels as he did his poems, never took them with complete seriousness or considered them his most valuable achievement. He had now reached a point of prosperity and fame when he could afford to give way to his lifelong desire to be known as a poet. Novels, though he expressed through them his sincerest convictions, were to him primarily the way by which he had earned his living since he had ceased to practise architecture. There was one more reason — a ludicrous but an actual one. Hardy, by instinct a recluse and a countryman, dreaded the social life into which he thought he was forced by the accident of being a popular novelist. Thinking so little of his fiction, he was agreeable to every suggestion of his publishers, and lived in horror of the day when they would order him to write a society novel! It was with real relief that he abandoned fiction forever.

Not only a series of volumes of poetry — many of the poems written long years before — now followed from his pen, but also the three parts of that masterly poetic drama, *The Dynasts*. Honors fell thick upon him; his public was growing up, and the furore over *Tess* and *Jude* was forgotten, or remembered with shame. In 1910 he received the Order of Merit, and in the same year something that he valued still more — the freedom of the city of Dorchester. He was showered with honorary degrees, from Oxford and Cambridge, from Aberdeen, Bristol, and St. Andrew's. He received the gold medal of the Royal Society of Literature. He became an honorary fellow of the Royal Institute of British

Architects — an honor, like his first architectural prize, probably more of a tribute to his literary than to his architectural renown. He was the third president of the Incorporated Society of Authors, the first two being Tennyson and Meredith. (Barrie — his intimate friend — succeeded him on his death.) During the war, as the only contribution he could make at his age, he served diligently as a local Justice of the Peace.

Before this, in 1912, the first Mrs. Hardy had died, rather suddenly, though she had long been weakening in health and apparently had had a premonition of her approaching end. Their marriage had been childless, but it had been a close and devoted union. In 1914, at 74, he married again; his second wife was his longtime secretary, a journalist and writer of children's books in her own right, Florence Dugdale, who later became his chief biographer. She was, of course, very much his junior, but she devoted herself to him rather as Watts-Dunton devoted himself to Swinburne, acting as companion, nurse, secretary, and, toward the end, perhaps a little as keeper of the museum. There is no doubt, however, that Hardy was extremely fond of her and happy in the fourteen years of his second marriage.

At the beginning of 1928, in spite of the care with which he was surrounded, he caught cold, and at his age the slightest illness proved fatal. His mind was clear to the last; the day before he died, he signed a check for the Royal Literary Pension Fund — the last time his hand held a pen — and on his very deathday he asked that his wife read him that stanza of the *Rubaiyat* which begins, "O Thou who man of baser Earth didst make." The stanza is an almost too perfect epitome of Hardy's own philosophy and of his attitude toward humanity.

Hardy's heart was removed and buried in his first wife's grave, near Dorchester; the remainder of his body was cremated and buried in the Poet's Corner in Westminster Abbey. On January 16th, five days after his death, there was an impressive memorial service there, attended by the most eminent men in England, and by thousands who came to do honor to one they revered. Few authors have had such tribute paid them so soon after their death.

In appearance, Hardy was under medium size (five feet, six and a half inches), slender, sandy-haired in youth, with blue-grey eyes and Roman nose. For years he grew a beard, but after 1890 wore only a mustache.

It was as a poet that he wished to be remembered, and it is possible that in the end his poetry will be felt to outweigh his prose. It is intellectual poetry, cryptic, sometimes difficult and gnomic, full of distinction and personal idiom, yet often beautifully lyric. He made no mistake in knowing himself for a poet.

If he had written only his earlier novels — that is, the series from *Under the Greenwood Tree* to *The Woodlanders* — it might be granted that his poems were his more valid contribution to English literature.

4

Yet these novels are so rich with the very soil of England, so penetrating in their psychology, so fresh and colorful, that they alone would have made any writer's fame. But it is the two books which brought down on their author the foul abuse of every bigot and dullard on three continents that are Thomas Hardy's great and unique achievement. Nowhere else in English fiction are to be found the profundity, the unification of feeling, the perfect presentation of great tragedy, that make *Tess of the d'Urbervilles* and *Jude the Obscure* immortal.

List of Major Works

1871. *Desperate Remedies*
1872. *Under the Greenwood Tree*
1873. *A Pair of Blue Eyes*
1874. *Far from the Madding Crowd*
1876. *The Hand of Ethelberta*
1878. *The Return of the Native*
1880. *The Trumpet-Major*
1881. *A Laodicean*
1882. *Two on a Tower*
1886. *The Mayor of Casterbridge*
1887. *The Woodlanders*
1888. *Wessex Tales*
1891. *A Group of Noble Dames*
1891. *Tess of the d'Urbervilles*
1892. *The Pursuit of the Well-Beloved*
1894. *Life's Little Ironies* and *A Few Crusted Characters*
1895. *Jude the Obscure*
1897. *The Well-Beloved* (re-written from 1892)
1898. *Wessex Poems*
1901. (dated 1902). *Poems of the Past and the Present*
1904. *The Dynasts*, Part I
1906. *The Dynasts*, Part II
1908. *The Dynasts*, Part III
1909. *Time's Laughingstocks and other Verses*
1910. *The Dynasts*, in one volume.
1913. *A Changed Man* (stories first published 1881-1900)
1914. *Satires of Circumstance*
1916. *Selected Poems*
1917. *Moments of Vision*
1922. *Late Lyrics and Earlier*
1923. *The Famous Tragedy of the Queen of Cornwall*
1925. *Human Shadows*
1928. *Winter Words* (poems published posthumously)

The World of Thomas Hardy

One of the clichés about the Victorian period is that it was a peaceful, complacent, intellectually stagnant period, a century of lethargy waiting to be demolished by the guns of World War I. Actually, the cliché is ridiculous to anyone even slightly acquainted with the nineteenth century. One might, in fact, argue the opposite case: the Victorian period was the most violent, most disturbed, most revolutionary period in the history of mankind. Without adopting either over-simplification, we may profitably take note of the vast changes which were occurring as a kind of backdrop for Hardy's works.

An Era of Change

The century is marked by change — in society, in politics, in religion, in art. Not the least of these changes was the change in the social structure, which resulted in shifts in political power. Nineteenth-century England was experiencing what modern economists call "take-off" — that emergence from rigid economic and political structures into the dynamic world of modern capitalism. For England, this change had begun back in the eighteenth century, but by Hardy's time the rapidity of the change was violent, almost chaotic. The effects of this change are well known: England was transformed from a rural and agricultural nation, with a population distributed fairly uniformly throughout the country, into an industrial and urban nation, with a population tending to gather, for better or worse, in the large cities. The causes of these tendencies and the laws of their operation are not yet completely understood.

Population Growth

Britain was the first modern country to be seriously concerned with a population explosion, locked as it was on two small islands. That concern may be seen as early as Adam Smith's *Wealth of Nations* (1776) and Thomas Malthus' *Essay on the Principle of Population* (1798), but the concern intensified throughout a century which saw Britain's population quadruple.

Urbanization

This population explosion, serious in itself, was aggravated by the collection of these masses of people in the new urban centers resulting from the factory system. In the eighteenth century, English textile industry was based on the work done in thousands of cottages in rural areas; while the farmer tended his small garden plot, family income might be supplemented by weaving done by his wife and daughters on small looms. With the invention of the power loom and related equipment, machinery became too unwieldy and too expensive for the individual farmer; the only people who could afford to operate and maintain the huge machines were the "Captains of Industry," the new "middle class," who could set up their equipment in central locations. The farmer, unable to support himself now without the additional income of his wife, was driven off the farm and into the city. Birmingham, Manchester, London, Liverpool, and many other large cities became huge dumping spots for millions of agricultural workers driven from the land.

Politics

The change in society naturally resulted in changes in political structure. It has been said that Victoria's reign proved that England could do without a monarch. Certainly the traditional institutions of king and royalty were being eroded. A new middle class of industrialist and merchant arose; shifts in population raised questions of reapportionment and demands for extension of the franchise to the middle class, later to the lower classes, and finally to women. In politics, as in society, change became a way of life, distasteful to many, but apparently unavoidable.

Religion

Such large external changes were paralleled by changes in ways of thinking, in attitudes, ultimately in the very character of the English people. Most critical here was the assault on traditional religion, either as represented in fundamental beliefs or through formal rituals and organizations. One may argue that the "romantic revolution" of the first part of the century had been an attempt to retain a "religious" or "illusioned" view of life. The progress of the rest of the century is in the direction of "dis-illusionment," or a casting-off — often regretfully — of religious interpretations of man and his place in the universe.

A New View of the Bible

For example, some Christians were concerned with the so-called "higher criticism" imported from Germany and France. This "higher criticism" called into question the traditional belief that the Bible was the "word of God," and was thus to be followed implicitly by the good Christian. Ernest Renan in France and David F. Strauss in Germany wrote influential books which attempted to "demythologize" the Bible by presenting an "historical Jesus." Matthew Arnold, among others in England, urged that the modern Christian rid himself of the superstitions and myths which had accumulated around the spirit of Christianity. During the Victorian period, then, men were examining, testing, and criticizing the Bible, that important source of God's revelation; for many men, this testing had shattering effects on their personal faith.

A New View of Nature

The other traditional proof of God's goodness was Nature: "the heavens declare the glory of God." Unfortunately this other refuge of belief was being destroyed by the advance of science. Many men could agree with Ruskin that their faith had been shattered by "the little hammers of the geologists." Each advance in biology and geology seemed to show more clearly that Nature was, in Tennyson's words, "red in tooth and claw." The laws of Nature, far from being beneficent to man or appearing controlled by a rational deity, seemed to work capriciously, even malevolently. Not only did individuals disappear, struck down by chance or accident, without any apparent purpose behind their brief lives, whole species appeared in the vast chronology of Time, lived briefly (in terms of millions of years), and were ruthlessly wiped out, again for no apparent reason.

Darwinism

The key figure here, of course, is Charles Darwin, whose *Origin of Species* (1859) must be recognized as one of the turning points in man's intellectual history. Actually Darwin's work is a culmination of the work of many others, "evolutionists" extending back into the eighteenth century. Although many of Darwin's conclusions have proved inadequate, *Origin of Species* is important because it is the first book which supported the evolutionary hypothesis with a mass of scientific data, evidence which Darwin had patiently accumulated for years. All other arguments — such as the sensational debates over man's descent from the monkey, or the existence of a "missing link" — are insignificant in comparison to the *evidence* which Darwin presented. It was difficult to deny that species were indeed mutable and that they seemed to change largely through accident in order to accommodate themselves to their environment. Furthermore, it seemed to many that God did not enter into this rather disorderly state of affairs. In the 1880's Nietzsche was to summarize the bleak situation with his agonized cry, "God is dead."

Disillusionment

Hardy reflects this agony of the nineteenth century in his novels. One might say that the key to his thinking is a "disillusioned view of life." Since there is no God to give meaning to life, Man is alone in the Universe, no better and no worse than other creatures who live or have lived for a brief moment on this speck called Earth. The Universe is neither malevolent nor benevolent; it is simply indifferent to the puny creature, Man, whose sufferings temporarily ruffle the environment. He is less a creature of Reason able to control his fate, to choose between Good and Evil, than a victim of forces within himself and outside himself. It is little wonder that his life is marred by unhappiness and apparent chaos; rewards are often given to the undeserving, and those who are good seem all the more tormented by the "slings and arrows" of life. In a world that is markedly unpredictable, it is difficult to find any measure of happiness; one can perhaps prevent total unhappiness by expecting little and by ridding oneself of all notions about self-fulfillment and one's importance in the scale of being.

Introduction to *Tess of the d'Urbervilles*

Tess may be looked upon as Hardy's attempt to write a classical tragedy in the form of a novel. But it is in some ways a measure of the stature of the book that it has been the subject of so much critical exegesis, and of so many different appraisals. To consider it as an impressionistic pastoral may seem at the least a limited view, but some readers have so regarded it. It has been criticized as insisting on the imposition of a rigid moral code on characters to whom it did not apply. And, to mention only one more general view, out of many, the book can be taken as the sublimation of all the characteristic late Victorian attitudes toward chastity, toward Christianity, toward justice, that are so familiar now in satire.

Nothing that might, or ought to be, said about *Tess* should be allowed to divert the reader from the unquestionable fact that *Tess*, like all of Hardy's last novels, is extraordinarily readable. After 75 years his books are read and enjoyed. That is the view to keep in sight. To many a young reader *Jude the Obscure* is THE novel; if it isn't *Tess* that has that place. To other readers, perhaps older, it is *The Return of the Native* or *The Mayor of Casterbridge*. For all of them, Hardy is a great novelist, always worth re-reading.

It may seem odd at first that a man who found the invention of incidents (but not, it must be emphasized, of plot) not only difficult but even a bit embarrassing, should have written so many books that have lasted and are actually read, not merely admired abstractly or listed dutifully in school histories of the novel. But those who are familiar with all of Hardy's books know that they are all permeated by his great and real humanity, his personal stature as a man, his anthropomorphism, his honesty and his sincerity. They are not, essentially, Victorian tracts, nor even criticisms of Victorian assumptions, but stories of people.

The reader, then, who enjoys Hardy's novels, tends to react to them as he does to his life and his era, affected strongly by some things, amused by others, indifferent, incensed, pleased, excited, disinterested, annoyed, or whatever. A girl of fifteen may lose her heart to *Tess*; a woman of sixty may find it too full of unrelieved misery for her taste. Thus, some may feel, for instance, that an understanding of *Tess* makes

9

British justice appear harsh and narrow, while others may think that it was so only in Tess' case, but by no means in all cases. And Angel Clare — are we to like him or condemn him; consider him a prig or a deceived honest man, a rebel or a hypocrite? Is it conceivable that to some modern readers Tess' whole story would seem more credible if Alec were a more attractive man? Whatever the case, *Tess*, which in its day was "quite contrary to avowed conventions," has not only survived several epochs of literary and social revolution, but has flourished and retained its ability to satisfy and nourish the modern mind.

Any book of Hardy's requires, of course, some discussion of Wessex, his fictitious name for a real part of England. Thomas Hardy is in a very real sense a part of the long, almost unique tradition of English nature writing, and the places *where* things happen to Tess are significant, as the events themselves are. The arrest of Tess at Stonehenge may be merely obviously symbolic, but the fruitfulness of the Valley of the Great Dairies has a real effect on Tess' spirits after the death of her baby, as the cozy rusticity of Marlott does when she is young.

Finally, mention must be made of Hardy's use of dialect speech. Whether he could have got the effects he achieved in his novels without the use of dialect (as Joyce, for example, imparts the precise rhythm and flavor of Irish speech without resort to phonetic spellings or Gaelic admixtures) is questionable; but at any rate, his ear for dialect has been warranted pure by scholars, and the words lend picturesqueness and verisimilitude to his books, and they are a characteristic mark of almost all of them.

Hardy's Philosophy

As a general rule, Hardy held that if man lived patiently and did not try to force his own will upon events, destruction could be avoided. Countryfolk, like John and Joan Durbeyfield and Marian, are creatures of animal instinct. They adapt and survive. They accept gain and loss, birth and death, luck and misfortune, with passive fatalism. They feel they can change nothing, and they accept responsibility for nothing, not even for the results of their own actions. The Durbeyfields cannot provide decently for their children, but that does not stop them from having them, nor does it drive them to greater efforts once the children are in need.

Tess accepts responsibility for things beyond her control, and that is what destroys her. She holds herself responsible for Prince's death, and the family hardships which result. It does not occur to her to blame her father, though had he not drunk himself into a stupor, the incident would not have occurred. Though Tess does not want to go to the "d'Urbervilles" at The Slopes, her sense of responsibility for her family eventually makes her go, thus setting the mechanism that will bring about her tragedy.

In some ways, Tess is an exception to Hardy's usual concept of character. In Hardy's view, to give way to an obsession was to invite disaster. To try to control and manipulate events was to set up a Promethean conflict — a conflict that courted the punishment of the gods. It is Alec's obsession with Tess that destroys him. Tess displays an extraordinary passivity in the face of the injustices that are done to her, but in an important way this works against her. Hardy tells us that had she made it more difficult for Angel Clare to abandon her, he would not have done so. Tess does fight to escape Alec, but at first she is too innocent, and finally she is too weakened by concern for her family. The fact that she gives in to him carries her further toward her destruction.

Thomas Hardy differs strikingly from many Victorian novelists in his attitude toward religion. In *Tess of the d'Urbervilles*, he attacks the churches and the clergy for making promises of redemption that he believes can not be fulfilled. In Hardy's view, God is an indifferent and unconscious force: mankind is at the mercy of an unheeding cosmos and "blind Chance" seems to be the will of the universe. Though the operation of chance is random and purposeless, man is totally powerless in the face of it. He will be thwarted by it, and to struggle against it is merely futile. (Note that while Hardy's "chance" is supposed to be indifferent, it seldom works in man's favor, and may, with much justification, be regarded as hostile to man.) Nothing is secure in such a world. For Hardy's characters, pain and suffering are the norm.

Hardy's chance-filled world, where human effort is repeatedly countered by malevolent forces, would seem unreal and absurd if he did not tell his stories in fable-like fashion. By invoking the timeless countryside and the ancient earth of Wessex, he succeeds in endowing their timelessness to his stories. By tying his narrative to the rhythms of the earth and making nature mirror the changing conditions and emotions of his heroine, Hardy shows Tess at one with the same immense forces which "sport" with her. The epic dimensions of these forces lend stature to Tess' efforts to overcome adversity.

Hardy fluctuates between fatalism and determinism. Fatalism maintains that all action is controlled by the nature of things or by Fate which is a great, impersonal, primitive force existing through all eternity, absolutely independent of human wills and superior to any god created by man. Determinism, while acknowledging that man's struggle against the will behind things is of no avail, recognizes that the laws of cause and effect are in operation. The human will is not free and the human being has no control over his own destiny, try as he may. The source of happiness is not within us, but rather rests with external manifestations of the universal force. Hardy sees life in terms of action, in the doomed struggle against the circumstantial forces against happiness. Incident plays an important role in causing joy or pain, and often an act of indiscretion in early youth can wreck the chances for happiness. Within a man's goodness may lie his own undoing; almost every step in Tess' undoing has its origin in a lofty motive and worthy trait of character.

The use of chance and coincidence as a means of furthering the plot was a technique used by many Victorian authors, but with Hardy it becomes something more than a mere device. Fateful incidents, overheard conversations, and undelivered letters symbolize the forces working against man in his efforts to control his own destiny. Many examples of the fateful incident may be found in *Tess*: Tess' misfortune to be born into a shiftless family; Durbeyfield's learning of his lineage; the death of the horse; the events which frustrate Tess's attempt to confess to Angel, ending in her letter slipping beneath the carpet; the death of her father; and the return of Angel just too late. One has the impression this is a book of "what might have been": if Angel had danced with Tess the first time he saw her, what a different story this would have been; if Angel had not caught sight of the portrait of the d'Urberville lady outside Tess's chamber, he probably would have weakened and entered the room with altogether different results; or if Tess had not overheard the conversation of Angel's brothers and had instead followed through on her plans to visit his parents, she probably would not have met Alec again and her entire life would have been changed.

Fate appears in the form of Nature, endowing it with varying moods which affect the lives of the characters. Those who are most in harmony with their environment are usually the most contented, and those who can appreciate the joys of Nature can find solace in it from their cares. But Nature can take on sinister aspects, becoming more of an actor than just a setting for the action: "The night came in, and took up its place there, unconcerned and indifferent; the night which had already swallowed up his happiness, and was now digesting it listlessly; and was ready to swallow up the happiness of a thousand other people with as little disturbance or change of mien." (Chapter 35)

Time is also used as a motif of fate. The joys of life are transitory and the moments of joy may be turned to bitterness by time, and love, that universal symbol of happiness, may be changed by time. For example, when Angel and Tess knew that "though the fascination which each had exercised over the other . . . would probably in the first days of their separation be even more potent than ever, time must attenuate that effect." (Chapter 36)

Woman is Fate's most potent instrument for opposing man's happiness. Closer to primitive feelings than man, woman is helpless in the hands of Fate and carries out Fate's work. In her search for love, the motivating passion of her life, woman becomes an agent in her own destiny. Tess and the dairymaids are vessels of emotion: "The air of the sleeping-chamber seemed to palpitate with the hopeless passion of the girls. They writhed feverishly under the oppressiveness of an emotion thrust on them by cruel Nature's law — an emotion which they had neither expected nor desired. . . . The differences which distinguished them as individuals were abstracted by this passion, and each was but portion of one organism called sex." (Chapter 23)

Perhaps the most ironic manifestation of Fate used by Hardy is that of convention. Convention and law can work as effectively against man as the other aspects of Fate, yet these are devised by man himself. Man is powerless to change the other workings of Fate; but those which are contrived by man and which work against him can be changed by man. Thus, we see in *Tess* a desperate cry against those evils which can and must be corrected. The social laws must be brought into accord with natural law. There are many examples of Hardy's rebukes against society and conventions. For example:

> She might have seen that what had bowed her head so profoundly — the thought of the world's concern at her situation — was founded on an illusion. She was not an existence, an experience, a passion, a structure of sensations to anybody but herself. To all humankind, Tess was only a passing thought. . . . Moreover, alone on a desert island would she have been wretched at what had happened to her? Not greatly. If she could have been created, to discover herself as a spouseless mother, with no experience of life except as a parent of a nameless child, would the position

have caused her to despair? No, she would have taken it calmly, and found pleasures therein. Most of the misery had been generated by her conventional aspect, and not by her innate sensations. (Chapter 14) ... She was ashamed of herself for her gloom of the night, based on nothing more tangible than a sense of condemnation under an arbitrary law of society which had no foundation in Nature (Chapter 41).

When Hardy concerns himself with the injustices of social law, Nature is portrayed as a positive thing. Joan says of Tess' pregnancy, " 'Tis nater after all, and what do please God!" Hardy says of Tess, "She had been made to break an accepted social law, but no law known to the environment [nature] in which she fancied herself such an anomaly.... But for the world's opinion those experiences would have been simply a liberal education."

To the Wessex rustic, Fate is also revealed by means of many omens and signs. Joan lives by her fortunetelling book, although she is afraid to have it in the house while she sleeps. Almost everything has significance: the cows will not give their milk, the butter fails to come in the churn, the cock crows in the afternoon. The vision of the d'Urberville Coach is a bad omen, as is the stone of the "Cross-in-Hand." Since Fate is a part of life, much can be explained away. Angel chooses Tess, but it is really Fate which has made the choice; therefore, the dairymaids do not blame Tess for any part of it. Marian says it must be something outside both Angel and Tess which has caused their separation, for she knows neither of them has any faults. It "was to be" that Alec should seduce Tess, that is, she is not to blame.

"My pessimism, if pessimism it be," wrote Hardy, "does not involve the assumption that the world is going to the dogs ... Whatever may be the inherent good or evil of life, it is certain that men make it much worse than it need be!"

Plot Summary

When Jack Durbeyfield, a poor peddler, learns that he is the descendent of the illustrious d'Urbervilles, he sees a chance of improving his position in the world. He and his wife, Joan, send Tess, their eldest daughter, to claim kin with the wealthy Mrs. d'Urberville. The Durbeyfields do not realize that Mrs d'Urberville is not a genuine d'Urberville. She is the widow of a wealthy merchant who assumed the name when he decided to settle in the country as a landed aristocrat.

At the d'Urberville estate, Tess meets young Alec d'Urberville. Attracted by her beauty, Alec determines to make a conquest of the girl. He writes to the Durbeyfields, offering Tess a job tending the fowls belonging to his mother. Mrs. Durbeyfield is impressed with Alec's flashy good looks and obvious wealth, and she persuades the reluctant Tess to accept.

When Tess meets Mrs. d'Urberville, she discovers that the old woman is blind. Alec continues his pursuit of Tess, and helps her family financially in order to gain the girl's confidence and gratitude. One night in the woods Alec seduces Tess.

Tess remains at the estate for only a short while longer, and then returns to her home in Marlott. She gives birth to Alec's child there, but the baby soon dies. In an effort to make a new life for herself, Tess leaves Marlott to work as a dairymaid at Talbothays Dairy.

The peaceful valley where Talbothays is situated gives Tess new hope and new vitality. She recognizes an apprentice dairyman there as a stranger who once lingered to watch her dance at the May Day festivities in Marlott. He is Angel Clare, youngest son of a minister. In spite of his family background, Angel declares himself an agnostic: he intends to become a farmer.

Angel is struck by Tess' innocent beauty and her quick adaptable mind. The two young people become friends, and their friendship deepens into love. Angel asks Tess to marry him, but at first she refuses. She believes that she is not good enough for him. Finally, Tess does consent, but her happiness is marred by her conviction that she should confess her past to Angel. When she tries to make him listen to her "confession," he refuses, telling her that they will confide in each other after the wedding.

On their wedding night, Angel makes his confession — telling Tess that he once had a brief affair with an older woman in London. Encouraged by his frankness, Tess forgives him and tells him about Alec d'Urberville. Horrified, Angel rejects her, and decides that they must part while he makes up his mind as to a future course of action. Angel tells her not to try to see him until he comes for her, but to let his parents know if she needs anything. He gives her some money and sends her to Marlott.

15

Neither Angel nor Tess reveals to anyone the true reason for their separation. Angel emigrates to Brazil where he intends to farm. Tess finds life unbearable in Marlott, and leaves after giving her parents half the money Angel left with her.

She takes what work she can find at farms and dairies. That work ends when winter comes, and she has only the remainder of the money Angel gave her to live on. That money is gone by the time a letter comes from Marian (a dairymaid friend) offering Tess work at Flintcomb-Ash. The two girls labor together through the winter in the turnip fields.

Unknown to Tess, Angel has lost both his health and his capital investment in Brazil. Tess does not hear from him, and finally she decides to visit his family. She walks long miles to the vicarage one Sunday, only to find the Clares are not at home. She goes to the church to wait for them, but overhears Angel's brothers discussing Angel's "unfortunate marriage." Humiliated, Tess leaves without waiting to see Mr. and Mrs. Clare.

On the way back to Flintcomb-Ash, Tess stops to rest near a barn where a wandering preacher is holding an audience spellbound. She is shocked when she comes face to face with the preacher and recognizes Alec d'Urberville. He follows her and tells her that his conversion was brought about by Mr. Clare, Angel's father. He says that he has forsaken his former evil ways and begs Tess to swear that she will never tempt him from his chosen path. It is plain that he is still attracted to her.

A few days later, Alec appears at Flintcomb-Ash and asks Tess to marry him. She tells him that she is already married, and begs him to leave her alone. She taunts him about his conversion, and questions his faith with arguments she learned from Angel. Alec gives up his preaching and blames Tess for his loss of faith. He persists in his attempts to win her, offering to care for her and her family. Tess desperately writes Angel, begging him to come and save her.

Shortly afterward, Tess' sister tells her that Mrs. Durbeyfield is seriously ill. Tess goes home and nurses her mother back to health. Though Joan recovers, Mr. Durbeyfield suddenly dies. The family is turned out of their cottage by the landlord. Alec reappears and again offers to help them, but Tess rejects him. The family packs up and goes to the town of Kingsbere. Alec follows them there, and again Tess sends him away.

In Brazil, Angel's misfortunes have given him a new maturity. He realizes how unjustly he has treated Tess, and sets sail for home. Illness delays him at the vicarage, and by the time he reaches Marlott, the Durbeyfields have gone. Angel follows them to Kingsbere. There, he finds Mrs. Durbeyfield, now living in comfortable circumstances. She reluctantly tells him that Tess is staying in Sandbourne.

Angel finally finds Tess, but a far different Tess than the one he knew. She is beautifully gowned, living in an elegant lodging. She tells him that he has come too late. His indifference and silence at last broke her will, and she has succumbed to Alec's persuasions. Heartbroken, Angel goes away. In a frenzy of grief, Tess stabs Alec to death.

Angel is walking toward the railway station when he sees Tess running to catch up with him. She is incoherent, but he understands that she is in trouble and takes her away with him. The two enjoy a blissful few days in a deserted house. Angel's plan is to walk until they reach a port where he can find a ship to take them safely away, but they are overtaken by the police at Stonehenge. Tess is arrested. Several months later she is hanged.

The plot of *Tess* is one of the simplest that Hardy ever devised: the woman sins, the woman pays. This plot was used by innumerable Victorian authors whose names will never be remembered. In the hands of Hardy, however, this hackneyed pattern is formed into a work of art. Hardy challenges two traditional themes: (1) the stain of unchastity can never be erased, and (2) the possibility of purifying atonement. By taking the sentimental pattern and coating it with irony, Hardy is able to evoke reactions to situations opposite to the usual ones.

Characters in the Novel

TESS DURBEYFIELD: A young, pure, beautiful and honest farm girl, the oldest of many children of somewhat improvident parents.

JACK DURBEYFIELD: Tess' father, whose natural aversion to work is intensified by the discovery that he is descended from an ancient noble family.

JOAN DURBEYFIELD: Tess' mother; once beautiful, like Tess, but neither as intelligent nor as principled as her daughter. She is like her husband in her easygoing ways.

LITTLE ABRAHAM: Tess' small brother; he serves merely to represent all of Tess' unnumbered and unnamed brothers and sisters.

'LIZA-LU: Tess' next younger sister. She symbolizes the pristine purity and idealism of the original unsullied Tess.

ALEC d'URBERVILLE: The son of Simon Stoke. His talents range from seduction to evangelical preaching.

MRS. d'URBERVILLE: The blind widow of Simon Stoke. She is mistress of "The Slopes," a mansion built by her husband after he retired from business in the North of England and assumed the name of the ancient d'Urbervilles.

ANGEL CLARE: Youngest son of the Reverend Mr. Clare of Emminster. Being too liberal in his thinking to prepare for the ministry, he turned to agriculture for a career.

THE REVEREND MR. CLARE OF EMMINSTER: Angel's father, a self-sacrificing clergyman of charitable sentiments but rigid opinions.

MRS. CLARE: Angel's mother, a kindhearted woman somewhat inclined to be swayed by the values of a class-conscious society.

FELIX CLARE: Angel's brother; a curate in a nearby town.

CUTHBERT CLARE: Angel's brother; a classical scholar and fellow of Trinity College.

MERCY CHANT: The daughter of the Clares' neighbor. She holds Bible classes and would like to have Angel marry her. Later, she marries Cuthbert Clare.

MR. CRICK: A kindly dairyman for whom Tess works.

MARIAN, IZZ HUETT AND RETTY PRIDDLE: Three dairymaids who are friends of Tess and who are in love with Angel Clare.

SORROW: Tess' child, who died in infancy.

Chapter Summaries and Commentaries

Phase the First: The Maiden

CHAPTER 1

Summary

Walking "somewhat to the left of a straight line," Jack Durbeyfield, a peddler with a fondness for drink, makes his way to the village of Marlott on a spring evening. Along the way he meets Parson Tringham, who greets him as "Sir John." Why does the parson address him in this fashion, asks the peddler, "when I be plain Jack Durbeyfield . . .?"

Parson Tringham is the historian and genealogist of the region. At first he shrugs off the "Sir John" as "only my whim," but then he confesses that while investigating the lineage of local families, he has learned that Durbeyfield is a direct descendant of Pagan d'Urberville, a French knight who came to England in 1066 with William the Conqueror. The d'Urbervilles once held manors all over Wessex, and were knighthood still handed down from father to son, Durbeyfield *would* be "Sir John." In Tringham's words, the d'Urbervilles "are extinct — as a county family." All that remains of their former grandeur seems to be the "wold silver spoon, and a wold graven seal" which their "debased" descendant Durbeyfield has in his possession at home.

Tringham goes on his way. Overcome by the news, Durbeyfield sits down by the roadside and falls into a reverie which is interrupted by Fred, a boy from the village of Marlott. Eager to share his new knowledge, Durbeyfield tells Fred of his "noble race," and his ancestors "in coats of mail and jewels, in gr't lead coffins weighing tons and tons." In keeping with all this reflected glory, he orders Fred to return to the Pure Drop Inn at Marlott, and send a horse and carriage to take the descendent of knights home.

As Fred is about to leave, the sound of a brass band is heard from the village. Fred reminds Durbeyfield that the May Day "women's club-walking," in which the peddler's daughter, Tess, is to participate, is about to begin. Durbeyfield decides to inspect this festivity when the carriage comes for him.

Commentary

The plot of *Tess of the d'Urbervilles* is motivated by a number of secrets revealed to the characters. In this chapter, we learn the first of the secrets that impels Tess' tragedy. The machinery for her destruction is set in motion when Parson Tringham tells Durbeyfield of his hitherto unsuspected noble ancestry. Durbeyfield, an unsophisticated countryman, has thought of himself as "no more than the commonest feller in the parish." Indeed, his habitual humility is conveyed to the reader by Hardy's description of the brim of his hat, which is thumb-worn from being doffed. When his humble image of himself is shattered by Tringham's news, the peddler is eager "to come into his own again." It is all too easy for him to forget the parson's advice to consider "how the mighty are fallen."

The first link in this tragedy is echoed in Parson Tringham's admission that "our impulses are too strong for our judgment sometimes." All through this book that same theme recurs — the conflict between impulse and thought, between passion and reason. Tringham regrets passing on his information, but it is already too late. Durbeyfield is exultant, and he lacks the judgment to control his impulses. The far-reaching effects of Tringham's discovery, however, will not strike down Durbeyfield, but his daughter, Tess. And at the close of the chapter, Tess is ready to come onstage as a participant in the May Day festivities.

"Wessex," Hardy's name for his native Dorset, is the scene of the novel. Its historical importance is hinted at when Parson Tringham tells Durbeyfield that "there are several families among the cottagers of this country of almost equal lustre." The region is crowded with the lore and traditions of British history: pagan peoples worshiped at Stonehenge (where the "sacrifice stone" will witness Tess' final sacrifice); Roman legions camped on Cadbury Hill; King Arthur may have lived, died, and been buried near Glastonbury Tor; King Alfred certainly defeated the Danish invaders on this dark and bloody ground. The importance of "Wessex" in Hardy's novels makes the place a "presence" rather than a mere setting. The people he wrote about seem to be an extension of this presence. For them, according to Hardy, life is hostile, and fate is indifferent and blind. But in this chapter, both fate and Wessex seem to smile on Durbeyfield. All about him is the balmy spring evening, the line of blue hills, the daisy-starred grass. It is indeed the calm before the storm.

Many of the words used by Hardy have their origin in Dorset dialect, and will probably be unfamiliar to most modern readers. A brief glossary of unfamiliar words will be included in the discussions of the chapters where they occur.

haggler: a peddler or huckster
vamp on: walk on
stripling: a lad
black-pot: sausage made of fat and blood

QUESTION: How can Durbeyfield's changed image of himself be expected to affect his family?

CHAPTERS 2 AND 3

Summary

Meanwhile, the women of Marlott prepare to honor the first day of May with their annual "club-walking." Hardy points out that this custom was once common all over England, a "survival from Old Style days, when cheerfulness and Maytime were synonyms." Dressed in white, the women and girls of the village walk two-by-two to the meadows, carrying peeled willow wands in one hand and white flowers in the other. Among them is Tess Durbeyfield, "a fine and handsome girl" of sixteen. Tess is pretty, an innocent girl who is, in Hardy's words, "at this time of her life a mere vessel of emotion untinctured by experience."

Along the way, the procession encounters the carriage containing Durbeyfield, drunkenly singing of his "gr't-family-vault-at-Kingsbere . . ." Tess is embarrassed at her father's conduct, but supposes that he is — as usual — merely drunk. However, she loyally threatens to leave the procession when her friends make fun of him.

Durbeyfield is forgotten when the women begin their customary dance in the meadow. The dance is part of the May Day celebration. At first the women dance with each other; later the village men will join them. Among the onlookers are three strangers, obviously young men of the upper classes. They are the Clare brothers — Angel, Cuthbert, and Felix — who are passing through Marlott on a walking tour. Cuthbert and Felix resume their hike, but Angel Clare lingers to join the dancing. He and Tess exchange glances, but never become partners, although both regret this. Shortly afterward, Angel leaves to catch up with his brothers. He is aware that Tess is gazing after him.

When the dancing is over, Tess remembers her father's "odd appearance" and goes home to see what has become of him. The interior of the Durbeyfield cottage provides a sad contrast to "the holiday gaities of the field." Tess' mother, Joan, is washing clothes and minding the six younger children. She tells Tess of Durbeyfield's newly-discovered connection with the illustrious d'Urberville family, but this exciting news is mixed with less happy tidings. Jack Durbeyfield has just come from the doctor who has told him that he has a heart condition. To celebrate his good news and console himself for the bad, Durbeyfield has gone to Rolliver's Inn, where he hopes "to get up his strength for his journey tomorrow with that load of beehives."

Tess is angered by this latest evidence of her father's shiftlessness. She offers to go and fetch him, but her mother undertakes the errand. Joan is only too happy to leave the younger children in Tess' care so that she can spend some time alone in her husband's company. It grows late, and neither parent returns. Tess sends her younger brother Abraham to fetch them. When he also fails to return, she sets out for the inn.

Commentary

Hardy points out that the May Day club-walking, which resembles to some extent the better-known custom of dancing around the Maypole, survives only in secluded country places like Marlott. He believes cheerfulness and Maytime are no longer possible in industrialized regions where "the habit of taking long views had reduced emotions to a monotonous average."

The celebration of the first of May probably originated in pre-Christian agricultural rituals, whose rites were meant to ensure fertility to the crops, as well as to livestock and humans. These ancient fertility rites were adapted in medieval and modern Europe to include a procession carrying trees, green branches, and garlands. Sometimes a May king or a May queen is appointed and a Maypole is set up. Hardy regrets that the people of Marlott seem to have forgotten the ancient pagan ways that gave May Day celebrations their meaning. For them, the club-walking has become a mere social custom.

In Chapter 2 we are introduced to Tess and Angel, the book's most important characters. Tess' white dress and Angel's name symbolize their innocence and purity.

Hardy has a flair for irony. When the upper-class Angel fails to choose her for a dancing partner, Hardy comments that Tess' d'Urberville ancestry doesn't even help her in "her life's battle" (Hardy's "Wessex" is always a battleground for his characters) "even to the extent of attracting to her a dancing-partner . . . So much for Norman blood unaided by Victorian lucre."

In Chapter 3, we meet Tess' mother, Joan Durbeyfield. She is a simple, rather silly woman, somewhat in awe of her oldest daughter. Perhaps this is because Tess has received an education. She has, we are told, "completed the Sixth Standard in National School" — the equivalent of graduating from high school. This is an unusual feat for a country girl of Hardy's time, and it brings out the fact of Tess' quick intelligence. In Chapter 30, Tess will tell Angel that her teachers said she "had great aptness, and should make a good teacher, so it was settled that I should be one. But there was trouble in my family; father was not very industrious and he drank a little." Perhaps there is some guilt in Joan's feeling for her daughter. Certainly Tess is more conscientious than her mother.

While Tess is a "modern girl" of the Victorian age, her mother is superstitious and old-fashioned. She consults the *Compleat Fortune-Teller*, an old book, when confronted with a problem. But the book is evidently of little help, for Hardy scornfully refers to "the shiftless house of Durbeyfield" and the six small children "entirely dependent on the judgment of the two Durbeyfield adults . . ." Are such conditions, he asks (mocking William Wordsworth), part of "Nature's holy plan?"

22

clipsing and cooling: clasping and embracing
poppet: doll, silly female
mommet: scarecrow, effigy
plim: to swell
mampus of volk: crowd of people
vlee: carriage
larry: noise, disturbance

QUESTION: How does Joan's superstitious nature influence her daughter's future?

CHAPTER 4

Summary

At Rolliver's Inn, a party of sorts is in progress upstairs. The landlady, Mrs. Rolliver, is entertaining several people, including the Durbeyfields, who are busily imagining a bright future for Tess. Mrs. Durbeyfield has learned that there is a wealthy woman named d'Urberville living near the village of Trantridge, not far from Marlott. She suggests sending Tess to visit this branch of the family to "claim kin," a move that might result in "some noble gentleman marrying her." At least, this is the fate foretold for Tess in Mrs. Durbeyfield's *Compleat Fortune-Teller*.

Tess herself arrives at this point. Her look is reproachful enough to make her father and mother collect Abraham from the place where he has been waiting on the stairway and leave for home. It becomes apparent that Jack Durbeyfield's condition will not permit him to undertake delivery of the beehives to Casterbridge, which is at least 20 miles distant over rough roads. Tess suggests that she and young Abraham go in his place. They reluctantly set out in the loaded family wagon, drawn by their horse, the aged and decrepit Prince.

As they jog along behind the old, slow horse, Tess and her brother drowse. They are rudely awakened when the mail-cart crashes into them and kills Prince. Stranded and waiting for help, Tess feels like a "murderess." She reproaches herself for her carelessness which has deprived the family of their "bread-winner." Without a horse, how can they get to market?

The problem is temporarily solved when a farmer conveys them first to market, and then back to Marlott with Prince in the wagon. Durbeyfield buries the horse in the garden, working harder to dig the grave than he does to feed his family. Because of their shiftlessness, Tess' parents are not as dismayed by the loss of the horse as she expects.

Commentary

Tess is obviously the strong member of the Durbeyfield family. They do not hesitate to load their burdens upon her shoulders. In spite of this, Hardy indicates that Tess (like her brother) is only a child, dismayed at the thought of claiming kin with a relative who might put her "in the way of marrying a gentleman."

The first ill omen connected with her "claiming kin" is the death of Prince. It will force her to try to retrieve the family "fortunes" by going to Trantridge. The dying horse splashes her with blood, foreshadowing a later tragedy.

Hardy's sense of despair at the indifference of the cosmos to human pain is echoed in the conversation about the stars between Abraham and Tess. Tess tells him that they live "on a blighted star." If they had been born on a "sound one," they would not have been so poor and unfortunate.

sumple: pliant, supple

QUESTION: Who bears the real responsibility for the death of Prince? Why?

CHAPTER 5

Summary

With the death of Prince, the condition of the Durbeyfields grows desperate. Racked with guilt at having "dragged her parents into this quagmire," Tess is nevertheless reluctant to visit the wealthy Mrs. d'Urberville in Trantridge. But when her father tells her he doesn't want her to go because "I'm the head of the noblest branch o' the family, and I ought to live up to it," she decides to go. "His reasons for staying away were worse to Tess than her own objection to going."

Tess has always carried a large share of the family burdens, and it has been a foregone conclusion that it would be she who would represent the family at the d'Urberville mansion in Trantridge.

When Tess reaches "The Slopes," Mrs. d'Urberville's country estate, she finds it a fine place, built "for enjoyment pure and simple, with not an acre of troublesome land attached to it . . ." Everything on the property speaks of money. Tess is dismayed and awed by its "new" appearance, and wishes she had not come.

At this point we learn that the d'Urbervilles who own all this are not truly members of the d'Urberville family. They are the family of Simon Stoke, a wealthy merchant who adopted the name of d'Urberville when he retired to the south of England. But to Tess this is still a secret — the second secret of the plot.

As Tess hesitates, Alec d'Urberville appears. He is a bold and handsome young man, who greets her in an overly familiar way. From him Tess hears that Mrs. d'Urberville is an invalid and cannot see her. Embarrassed, Tess pours out the story of the supposed kinship between her family and his. Attracted by the girl's innocence and beauty, Alec tries to impress her by showering her with hothouse flowers — roses. He promises to try to find a place for her in the household on the condition that she refer to herself as Tess Durbeyfield: there must be "no nonsense about d'Urberville." Alec's intentions, however, are not so benign as they seem. When Tess leaves, he chuckles in anticipation of his next meeting with this pretty "cousin."

Commentary

The name of d'Urberville is further "debased" when the newly rich Stokes adopt it. Hardy ironically points out that the Stokes form "a very good stock whereon to regraft a name which sadly wanted such renovation." There is more sad "renovation" in the way the Stokes have forced back the ancient woodland known as The Chase to build their countryhouse. In Hardy's view, the upstart Stoke-d'Urbervilles are true barbarians intent on changing the nature of the countryside and its people.

Hardy's concept of an indifferent Nature is underscored in this chapter: "Nature does not often say 'See!' to her poor creature at a time when seeing can lead to happy doing; . . ." Nature does not warn Tess that she is "doomed to be seen and coveted that day by the wrong man [Alec]," while to the right man she is still but "a transient impression." And it is Nature that gives Tess her "luxuriance of aspect, a fullness of growth, which made her appear more of a woman than she really was . . ." and belies her youth and innocence.

Tess cannot know yet that this swarthy, sensual young man represents the "tragic mischief" that will ruin her life.

crumby: plump, comely, buxom
Malthusian: pertaining to the view of political economist Rev. T. R. Malthus (1766-1834) that poverty is inevitable unless population increase is checked
pollarded: a way of cutting trees to promote dense foliage

QUESTION: What does Hardy suggest about Alec d'Urberville's character when he refers to him as "the swarthy Alexander?"

CHAPTERS 6 AND 7

Summary

When Tess returns home, a letter has already reached her mother from Mrs. d'Urberville. It offers the girl a job at The Slopes tending fowls. Tess is doubtful and suspicious of the offer. She prefers to stay in Marlott and to try to find work there, but her efforts to find a job in the neighborhood are unsuccessful. An unexpected visit from Alec d'Urberville further weakens her determination to stay home.

Her mother, convinced that the fowl-tending is just Mrs. d'Urberville's "artful way" of introducing the girl into the Stoke family without raising her hopes, urges Tess to return to Trantridge. In spite of her misgivings about Alec, Tess finally agrees. Perhaps she can earn enough money at Trantridge to buy a new horse for her family.

Upon agreeing to take the job, Tess is informed by a letter (written in a rather masculine hand) that a cart will come to take her and her luggage to Trantridge. On the morning of her departure, her mother (perhaps dreaming of a marriage between Tess and Alec) insists the girl heighten her beauty by donning her best frock. But as the time for Tess' leave-taking draws near, her lovely innocence seems to stir some misgivings in Joan Durbeyfield. She accompanies Tess to the point where the cart is to meet her.

When the cart arrives, only Tess' luggage is put aboard it. "A spick and span gig" (a light one-horse carriage) driven by Alec intercepts the girl. After some hesitation, Tess gets into the gig. She is driven away, and as she disappears, her mother belatedly wonders about Alec's true character. Should she have let her daughter go with this bold young man? However, when she later discusses the incident with her husband, she consoles herself with the thought that the young man is in love with Tess. She decides Tess will be all right "if she plays her trump card aright." When Jack Durbeyfield asks if the trump card is her d'Urberville blood, Joan replies, "No, stupid; her face — as 'twas mine."

Commentary

As we shall see, the pressure Tess' family puts upon her is another force that drives her to her doom. Her going to Trantridge is one more of the many sacrifices she will make. Her sense of guilt (at this point, guilt over the death of the horse) is another factor in her tragedy.

Mrs. Durbeyfield is a shallow woman who relies heavily on appearances. When Alec dazzles her with his diamond ring, she at once assumes he is a good catch for Tess. The girl's own likes or dislikes are not important to Joan Durbeyfield. She feels that Tess must use her sexual attraction to secure Alec, philosophizing that "if he don't marry her afore he will after. For that he's all afire wi' love for her any eye can see." It is easy to see that Tess' moral principles are superior to her mother's.

lammicken: lambkin; a young lamb, used as a term of endearment

QUESTION: Why does Joan Durbeyfield regard Tess' beauty as more important than her d'Urberville blood to her future prospects?

CHAPTER 8

Summary

As Tess rides beside Alec, he begins to drive the gig with reckless speed. As they descend a long, steep hill, the gig goes even faster. Tess, nervous about travelling on wheels since the accident with her father's horse, clutches at Alec's arm, but he insists that she hold him around the waist. At the bottom of the hill she lets go of him, angry at the advantage he has taken of her momentary fear. To force her to embrace him once more, Alec speeds up the horse when they approach the next hill. This time, in spite of the jolting, swaying carriage, Tess refuses to hold on to him. Alec then promises to slow down if he may kiss her, and the shaken girl desperately agrees.

When Alec kisses her, Tess wipes away the caress with her handkerchief. Her unconscious act angers Alec, and he starts racing again at the next downhill stretch. This time, he tells her, he will not stop unless she agrees to a second kiss that must not be wiped away. Tess bows to his demand, but avoids the kiss because at that moment her hat blows off. She asks Alec to let her dismount and fetch it. Then she refuses to get back into the gig, stating that she will walk the remaining miles to Trantridge.

Realizing that the hat was only a ruse, Alec curses her. Shocked at his language, Tess tells him that she hates him. Her anger dampens Alec's and makes him laugh. He promises to behave himself if only she will get back in the gig, but Tess has no confidence is his word. She walks on, wondering if she should return home instead. But the thought of her family's need for her earnings keeps her moving toward Trantridge. The disgruntled Alec drives the carriage along beside her until they reach his home, The Slopes.

Commentary

Alec's attempt to frighten Tess into submission shows us another side of his character. His desire for the girl makes him reckless and overbearing, but he is genuinely contrite when his actions cause Tess discomfort or inconvenience, such as forcing her to walk to the estate. He wants to master her, but he respects the pride that causes her to react to his tactics with anger. (It is interesting to the reader that Alec is the only character in the novel who can provoke Tess to wrath.)

Although Alec sincerely wants Tess to like him, he repels her with his arrogance and coarseness. Her character is more refined than his. When he sneers that she is "mighty sensitive for a cottage girl" after she wipes away his kiss, he only proves that he is insensitive. In spite of his adoption of the d'Urberville name, Alec is unable to adopt the manners that should belong to aristocracy. He lacks Tess' nobility of spirit.

QUESTION: Can you pick out at least two descriptive passages in this novel that indicate Alec's sensual nature?

CHAPTER 9

Summary

At The Slopes, Tess becomes acquainted with the poultry farm she is to supervise. It consists of a cottage in an enclosure, both much in need of altering and improving. While Tess is looking over her surroundings, one of the manor servants comes to take her to Mrs. d'Urberville, adding that the old lady "wants the fowls as usual." The servant also tells her that Mrs. d'Urberville is blind.

Tess takes two fine Hamburgh cocks under her arms and follows the servant to Mrs. d'Urberville's room in the manor house. The old lady greets her, then takes the fowls. She identifies them by touch, calls them by name, and then repeats the process with all the fowls in Tess' care. Satisfied, she asks if the girl can whistle tunes. Tess admits she can — after a fashion. Mrs. d'Urberville tells her she must practise every day so that she can whistle to her pet bullfinches. The birds learn to sing the tunes they hear.

The servant remarks that Alec had whistled to the bullfinches that morning, but the old lady does not seem pleased at the news. Though there appears to be little affection between mother and son, this is not actually so on Mrs. d'Urberville's part. She loves her son dearly, but she is not blind to his faults.

Later in the day, Tess makes a few feeble attempts to whistle. Alec overhears her, and offers to teach her how — promising to keep his distance. Grateful, Tess finds her anger with him is dissipating. One day, as she is whistling to the birds, she spies the toes of a pair of boots beneath a curtain. After that she checks the curtains each morning, but Alec has apparently had second thoughts and does not return. Tess begins to feel more at ease at The Slopes, but still she does not really trust Alec.

Commentary

Tess' awe of Mrs. d'Urberville is reflected in her impression of the fowl-presenting as a "Confirmation, in which Mrs. d'Urberville was the bishop, the fowls the young people presented . . ." Although the old lady presides regally over "the community of fowls," she seems to have little control over her son, of whom she is "bitterly fond." Although Alec's mother may be blind in fact, she is not blind in regard to Alec. Yet, curiously, she does not warn Tess against him — perhaps because she is blind to Tess' beauty. Perhaps, also, she feels the girl is safe behind the wire netting around the cottage. Even Alec seems to respect this barrier.

QUESTION: How does Alec manage to remove most of Tess' "original shyness of him?"

CHAPTER 10

Summary

The young working people of the Trantridge area enjoy spending their Saturday nights at the nearby market town of Chaseborough. There they drink, dance, and enjoy themselves. Urged by her fellow workers, Tess finally agrees to go on one of these outings, and finds it pleasant. From then on she goes often, but she always makes sure of the protective company of her fellow workers when it is time to return to Trantridge.

One Saturday night in September she waits for them in vain. When they fail to appear, she goes to look for them and finds them in the midst of a wild revel at a local hay trusser's barn. At this point, Alec d'Urberville appears and offers to drive Tess home, but she refuses. She waits until her friends finally begin to straggle back along the road to Trantridge. But as Tess walks along with them, trouble brews. Car Darch, a Trantridge girl known as "the Queen of Spades" to her friends, begins a quarrel by saying that Tess thinks herself better than the rest because Alec d'Urberville fancies her. Car tries to provoke physical combat with Tess, who refuses and begins to edge away.

At this moment Alec appears on horseback, and demands that the workers tell him the reason for the row. They offer no explanation, so he urges Tess to jump up behind him and "get shot of the screaming cats in a jiffy." Tess does so because she is frightened by the surly mood of her companions. As she rides away with Alec, Car Darch's mother looks after her, saying, "Out of the frying pan into the fire!"

Commentary

Mrs. Darch's observation is all too accurate. Tess would have been far safer with the "screaming cats" than with Alec. What is about to happen to her is foreshadowed by the bacchanalian revel in which her friends are compared by Hardy to Pan and Syrinx, and Priapus and Lotis. (According to Greek mythology, Priapus was the god of male generative power; Pan the pastoral god of fertility. Syrinx and Lotis were nymphs pursued by these two gods. The reference to Alec's pursuit of Tess is clear.)

The reader should note that Car Darch is jealous of Tess because she (Car) used to receive Alec's attentions. Tess is to be only one of his many conquests, but as the story will show, she will be the most important and consequential one.

QUESTION: What does Hardy mean when he writes "fear and indignation at these adversaries could be transformed by a spring of the foot into a triumph over them" in referring to Tess' acceptance of Alec's offer to take her home on his horse?

29

CHAPTER 11

Summary

As they ride through the night, Alec asks Tess why she seems to dislike his kissing. Tess replies that she supposes it is because she does not love him. His attempts at love-making are offensive to her. In spite of the fact that he has rescued her from an unpleasant situation, she is dubious about him. But she is also exhausted, and she fails to notice that Alec has allowed his horse to stray so that they miss the turnoff point for Trantridge. He has done this deliberately in order to prolong their time together, but fog has enveloped them and Alec is no longer sure of his location.

Tess has been drowsing, but suddenly she awakes and realizes that they are near The Chase — "the oldest wood in England" — and far from the track leading homeward. She calls Alec "treacherous" and demands that he let her dismount so that she can find her way alone. Alec agrees on the condition that she rest beneath the trees while he checks on their position. Because she is really too tired to go further, Tess settles herself on a bed of leaves. Alec gives her his coat to protect her from the cold. Before setting off to reconnoiter, he tells her that her father now has a new horse, and her brothers and sisters have new toys — thanks to him. His generosity touches Tess, and she relaxes as he leaves her. When he returns, she has fallen asleep. What follows, in Hardy's words, "was to divide our heroine's personality thereafter from that previous self of hers . . ."

Commentary

With this chapter, both the first Phase of the book and Tess' innocence come to an end. The darkness that contributed to the loss of the family's horse (and thus sent Tess to Trantridge) is like the darkness that shrouds Alec's conquest of Tess. Hardy's sense of fate and retribution is present in the suggestion that Tess may be suffering the same fate her knightly ancestors dealt out to peasant girls. "But though to visit the sins of the fathers may be a morality good enough for divinities, it is scorned by average human nature; and it therefore does not mend the matter."

Tess' innocence, which has so attracted Alec (later in the book she says that she didn't know what Alec was doing until it was too late) is reflected in Hardy's imagery in this chapter. Tess' outline, glimmering through the night, is called "nebulous," "of a dreamlike quality." But the dream has turned into a nightmare from which there is no awakening.

The strange ambiguity of Alec's nature makes Alec want to help Tess at the same time he wants to ruin her. When he obeys his better impulses and is generous to her family, he awakens her gratitude and weakens her resistance to him. But he cannot help taking advantage of this hold over her, and so he destroys any affection she might have had for him. This flaw in his character will prove fatal for them both.

QUESTION: Why do you think Hardy used the ancient primeval woods as a setting for this chapter?

Phase the Second: Maiden No More

CHAPTERS 12 AND 13

Summary

A few weeks after that night in the forest, Tess is walking along the road at dawn, carrying her few possessions. She has left the d'Urberville household forever. Her "experience" with Alec makes it impossible for her to remain. When she reaches the incline near Marlott down which Alec drove so wildly months ago, she finds Alec again waiting beside his gig. He abuses her, demanding to know why she left The Slopes without telling anyone. Does she intend to return? Tess says she cannot.

Alec offers to drive her the rest of the way home. Tess rides beside him, but when Marlott comes into view, she begins to cry. She sobs that she wishes she were dead. Her submission to Alec's passion would have been excusable, she says, if she loved him. But as it happened, it was only a despicable "weakness" on her part. Alec offers to provide for her "to the uttermost farthing," but she scornfully refuses his money. He tells her that she is too "high and mighty," and admits that he "was born bad, and I have lived bad, and I shall die bad in all probability." But he promises to never again be bad to Tess and assures her he will give her any help she asks for.

Tess dismounts from the gig, and coldly permits him to kiss her on the cheek in farewell. Although Alec urges her to reconsider and go with him, she refuses. She sets out on foot toward Marlott. On the way she meets a sign painter. He does most of his work on Sundays, he tells Tess, and soon she understands why when she sees him painting "THY, DAMNATION, SLUMBERETH, NOT." on a fence. Horrified by the text, Tess says she cannot "believe God said such things." The painter tells her that his work is inspired by the Reverend Clare of Emminster — a name that is to have future repercussions for Tess.

When the girl reaches home, her mother asks if she has returned to be married. When Tess tells her what has happened, Mrs. Durbeyfield is vexed because Tess has not gotten Alec to marry her — thus "doing some good for your family instead o' thinking only of yourself." Tess realizes then that Alec never mentioned marriage, and wonders whether she would have been weak enough to accept such a proposal. She decides she would not, and reproaches her mother for not telling her more about the facts of life, thus preparing her for the "danger in menfolks." Mrs.

Durbeyfield admits she is partly to blame for her daughter's predicament, and resigns herself to making the best of it.

For a time, Tess is the center of interest in Marlott. Her friends good-humoredly envy her for her supposed conquest of Alec. But Tess suspects that she is being gossiped about, and she sinks into depression. From then on she remains indoors during the day, going out only after dark in the solitary woods. Now the darkness that contributed to her ruin becomes her friend, hiding her from curious stares. Her pregnancy knits her closely to nature. She thinks the wind reproaches her, the rain expresses "irremediable grief at her weakness . . ." But the "accepted social law" Tess has broken is more important to her than to her neighbors.

Commentary

For Tess' mother and her neighbors, her fall from grace and her pregnancy were simply "Nater" (nature) — a state of affairs that "do please God." Tess herself reflects some of this primitive philosophy when she recoils from the lurid Biblical text put up by the sign painter. For these country people who live so close to nature, following impulse is "natural." Over and over, Hardy comments on the clash between "natural impulse" and reason; between man, nature, and society.

Unhappily, Tess is too submerged by guilt to appreciate the possible tolerance of her friends and family. She is surrounded by "a cloud of moral hobgoblins" that terrifies her "without reason." She hides in the darkness, which she no longer fears, and shuns the daylight of social convention. The sign painter, whose Biblical texts seem to Tess to accuse her, is part of this "daylight."

Notice that Tess' pride makes her call her submission to Alec a "weakness," even though her "eyes were dazed by [Alec] for a little." Her honesty is more important to her than any material gain marriage with Alec might have brought her. It is her honesty and pride that make her refuse his help and blame herself for having "succumbed to adroit advantages he took of her helplessness."

QUESTION: How does Hardy show us the change in Tess before and after her affair with Alec?

CHAPTERS 14 AND 15

Summary

Time passes. By the following August, Tess has become a mother. Her bitter experiences have transformed her from a girl to a woman, "the same, but not the same; at the present stage of her existence living as a stranger and an alien here, though it was no strange land that she was in."

Tess has joined the other women of the village to work in the fields.

Her daily labors are interrupted by the arrival of her brothers and sisters who bring her the baby to be fed. Tess' feelings toward her child are mixed: she both loves and hates it. She holds it "with a gloomy indifference that was almost disdain" — then falls to kissing it passionately. Her fellow workers discuss her with sympathy. One of them says that it was "a thousand pities that it should have happened to she, of all others." Their kindness seems to cheer her. On the way home from work, she is almost happy until she learns that her child has become desperately ill during the afternoon. It soon becomes plain that the baby will die, and Tess remembers that it has never been baptized. She begs her father to send for the parson, but Mr. Durbeyfield refuses because he is sensitive to "the smudge which Tess had set upon" his noble ancestry. Tess baptizes the child herself by candlelight, with her brothers and sisters as witnesses. The name she gives her infant is, fittingly, "Sorrow."

When the child is dead, Tess gets the vicar's reluctant permission to bury it in the church cemetery, in a corner "where all unbaptized infants, notorious drunkards, suicides," and other outcasts are laid to rest.

Tess remains at home through the winter, but she now realizes she can no longer be comfortable in Marlott. In her misery she holds herself so aloof from village life that almost everyone forgets about her baby and her troubles. With the spring comes new hope, for she hears of a job as dairymaid at a farm "many miles to the southward." She hopes that by taking this job she can shrug off her troublesome present identity and become plain Tess, the dairymaid. Perhaps then she can sever her connections with "d'Urberville air-castles." But this is easier said than done, for the dairy farm to which she is going is near some of the former estates and family vaults of the ancient d'Urbervilles. Perhaps, she thinks, being in her "ancestral land" will bring her luck at last.

Commentary

Hardy's intense feeling for Nature is apparent in these two chapters. When Tess is working in the field, she becomes "a portion of the field; she has somehow lost her own margin, imbibed the essence of her surroundings, and assimilated herself to it." She becomes "part and parcel of outdoor Nature."

Tess responds to the rhythm of the seasons. It was spring when she went to Trantridge, full of hope. Alec seduced her in the fullness of summer, and autumn brought her a harvest of guilt and despair. For her, winter was a time of frozen misery. But when spring comes again, Tess is ready to live again, to try for a new beginning.

To Hardy, the Industrial Revolution was a monster that destroyed the traditions and meaning of country life. His despair is revealed in his description of the passage of the mechanical reaper along the field in which Tess works. Its automatic progress either destroys or drives to cover all that is part of Nature.

QUESTION: What does the phrase "unexpended youth" tell us about Tess' state of mind as she sets off for the dairy farm?

Phase the Third: The Rally

CHAPTERS 16 AND 17

Summary

Tess arrives at Talbothays, the dairy farm, on a May morning. Her experiences during the "silent, reconstructive years" since Trantridge have matured her, and she is able to think with scorn of her entombed "useless ancestors." "I have as much of mother and father in me!" she thinks, "and she was only a dairymaid." The valley where Talbothays is located is "drawn to a larger pattern" than Tess' native Blackmoor Vale, and the sight of its expanse rekindles her spirits.

Once at Talbothays, she is put to work milking cows under the supervision of Mr. Crick, the master dairyman. To make the milk "come down," the milkers sing an old ballad to the cows. Their performance brings forth a comment from one of their co-workers, who proves to be Angel Clare. Tess recognizes him as the wayfarer who failed to choose her as his partner at the May Day dance, but Angel does not remember her. He is at Talbothays to learn the business of dairying so that he can take up the life of a farmer. Izz and Marian, the dairywomen with whom Tess shares a room, tell her that Angel is the son of a parson who is "the earnestest man in all Wessex." The young man, in their words, is "too much taken up wi' his own thoughts to notice girls."

Commentary

The descriptions of the difference between Blackmoor Vale and the Valley where Talbothays is located play a double role. They symbolize the difference between Tess' past mental state and the "rally" of her "invincible instinct towards self-delight." They also symbolize the difference between Alec (Blackmoor Valley) and Angel Clare (the Valley of Talbothays). Blackmoor is "luxuriant," a place with rivers where the unwary "might sink and vanish . . . ." By contrast, the air of the Valley of the Great Dairies is "clear, bracing, ethereal," and the waters of its river are "clear," "pure" with "pebbly shallows." Like them, Angel is pure, with a clear, ethereal intellect — but he has his shallows in which the unwary may founder.

QUESTION: How is Angel Clare made to seem different from the other dairy workers?

34

CHAPTER 18

Summary

Angel Clare's appearance and background are given in this chapter. In Hardy's own words, there is something "nebulous, preoccupied, vague" about him. He is the youngest son of the Reverend James Clare, a poor parson — the same parson who inspired the sign painter in Chapter 12. Angel's parents had supposed that he would study for the ministry, as his brothers had done. But Angel had serious doubts about his father's professed faith. He became an atheist and, as a consequence, the Reverend Clare refused to spend money on his wayward son's education at Cambridge University. After drifting without direction for a few years, Angel decided to become a farmer, because farming seemed to him a "vocation which would probably afford an independence without the sacrifice of what he valued ... intellectual liberty." Since making this decision, he has been serving apprenticeships at selected farms to learn the various skills he will need.

Now, at the age of twenty-six, he has come to Talbothays as a boarder and an apprentice dairyman. There he has come to enjoy the company of his fellow workers and the out-of-doors life. "He grew away from old associations, and saw something new in life and humanity," wrote Hardy. He began to notice Tess a few days after her arrival, first becoming aware of her "fluty voice." Her "fresh and virginal" appearance is very appealing to him, and he begins to wonder if he has not met her somewhere before.

Commentary

Although Angel and Tess come from different walks of life, they have many things in common. Both have disappointed their parents' hopes for them. Both have suffered a "disgrace" — in Angel's case, it is atheism. Both respond to nature and to music. Both have an intelligence and awareness beyond their education. Certainly, Tess' metaphysical speculations about sending her soul forth from her body are not the thoughts one would expect a dairymaid to voice. Both have had a disastrous sexual experience; Angel's revulsion after an affair with a woman in London will later influence his relationship with Tess.

It is interesting to note that Angel shares Thomas Hardy's "unconquerable, and almost unreasonable, aversion to modern town life ..." Hardy is obviously expressing his own opinions when he writes that the outdoor life at Talbothays makes Angel "wonderfully free from the chronic melancholy which is taking hold of the civilized races with the decline of belief in a beneficent Power." That beneficent Power would never have authorized the sign painter's threatening texts.

Angel discovers some of his fellow human beings to be "mutely Miltonic, some potentially Cromwellian ..." The first reference is to

John Milton, the English poet (1608-1674), and refers to the imaginative power that characterized his work. The second refers to Oliver Cromwell, the Puritan Lord Protector of England (1599-1658), and a man of stern virtue who became cruel and intolerant when forced into a position beyond his talents.

The "Article Four" that Angel refused to "underwrite" is one of the Thirty-nine Articles in the doctrine of the Church of England that its ministers must swear by. This particular Article refers to the resurrection of Christ, and holds that after rising from the tomb, Christ again assumed human form.

QUESTION: What is Angel's opinion of rank and wealth?

CHAPTER 19

Summary

Mr. Crick wants to prevent his cows from preferring one milker to all the others. Although he makes it a practice to interchange both cows and milkers daily, Tess begins to find that her favorite cows are being constantly lined up for her. This turns out to be Angel's doing. When Tess chides him, Angel replies that it is all right because "You will always be here to milk them." Although Tess hopes she is going to be permanently based at Talbothays, she worries that Angel thinks *he* is the reason she wants to stay there. Angry with herself for giving such an impression, she goes for a walk in the garden that evening.

The notes of a stringed instrument attract her attention, and she discovers Angel also walking about, playing a harp. The two enter into conversation and discover that they see many things in the same light. "This hobble of being alive is rather serious," says Angel, surprised when Tess confesses to a fear of "life in general." He is impressed by her seriousness, and the depth of her feeling. But Tess, wondering why so well-educated a young man should want to be a farmer, feels quite inferior to him. "When I see what you know, what you have read and seen and thought, I feel what a nothing I am!" she tells him. He offers to teach her anything she would like to know, but she replies that "books will not tell me" such things as "why the sun do shine on the just and the unjust alike."

Tess wonders if he might be more impressed with her if she told him of her noble d'Urberville ancestors. She indirectly seeks Mr. Crick's opinion of such a revelation. Mr. Crick tells her that Angel "can't stomach old families," and Tess decides to hold her tongue and enjoy this new friendship in these happy new surroundings.

Commentary

The setting in which Angel and Tess first talk at length is an ominous one — the ruined edge of a garden where colorful weeds give off offensive smells. The place seems like a decadent version of the lush garden at The Slopes, where Alec heaped roses on Tess, and, symbolically, its slime and blight stain Tess as she moves through it. Perhaps Hardy intended this place to symbolize the Garden of Eden, barred to mankind forever by an angel with a flaming sword. But the angel Tess finds here has a harp, not a sword. With his intelligence and his offer to teach her, he draws her into a happy dream where she is "conscious of neither time nor space."

rozums: persons with strange ideas

QUESTION: Why does Tess at first regard Angel "as an intelligence rather than as a man?"

CHAPTER 20

Summary
The attraction between Tess and Clare grows until they are "balanced on the edge of a passion." They meet constantly; they study each other, but they have not yet made commitments to one another.

It is Tess' task to arouse the milkers for work, and she makes a point of waking Angel first in the early pre-dawn hours. They meet out-of-doors, and in the "luminous gloom," seem like apparitions to each other. At such times, Angel envisions Tess as a goddess, and calls her by such names as Demeter and Artemis. "Call me Tess," she begs, for she does not like names which she cannot understand. As it grows lighter, Tess loses her ethereal beauty and is no longer a goddess, but a beautiful mortal "who had to hold her own against the other women of the world."

Commentary
The "luminous gloom" of midsummer pre-dawn makes Tess seem "a divinity who could confer bliss" rather than a mortal "who craved it." These hours make Angel think of the Resurrection hour, and Hardy points out with grim irony, "He little thought the Magdalen might be at his side." With this comment he reminds us of the tragedy that awaits the lovers. They seem to sense it too, for they struggle to keep apart. But their destinies are "converging under an irresistible law." Hardy also reminds us, by referring to the lovers as Adam and Eve, that the "fruit of knowledge" (of Tess' past) will be eaten by Angel, and both will be driven from their Eden.

QUESTION: How does Hardy show us that Angel idealizes Tess?

CHAPTERS 21 AND 22

Summary
One morning, the milk will not turn into butter, no matter how hard

it is churned. Mr. Crick is reminded of a story about a local milker named Jack Dollop who seduced a milkmaid and then refused to marry her. When her mother arrived to demand justice, Dollop hid in his churn and was battered when the girl's mother began to churn vigorously. The beating he received forced him to surrender and to agree to marry the girl. All the dairyfolk except Tess find this local legend amusing, but to her it is too reminiscent of her own past.

Mrs. Crick suggests that the butter will not come because someone in the house is in love (a local superstition). Depressed and embarrassed, Tess leaves the milkhouse — and at that moment the butter does come.

Later, when Tess has retired, she overhears the girls who share her room talking about Angel Clare. All agree they would gladly marry him if only he would choose one of them, but "he likes Tess Durbeyfield best." The news does not cheer Tess. Ought she allow Angel to be interested in her, to let any man marry her?

Morning brings another minor calamity to the dairy. The butter is discovered to taste of garlic weeds, and all the milkers set out for the meadows to uproot the offending plants. Angel walks with Tess, who tries to interest him in the other dairymaids, praising their talents and charms. But she cannot make herself say, "Marry one of them . . . and don't think of marrying me." She resolves to try to stay away from him, and so to give the other girls their chance. But in spite of the fact that the girls encourage him, Angel's behavior is circumspect. Tess feels new warmth and respect for this man who takes such pains to say or do nothing that might injure their reputations.

Commentary

Everything seems to conspire against Tess' good intentions. Her attempt to interest Angel in her co-workers is doomed in the lush valley where conjurers can bring the butter, and the morning dew can turn a mortal into a goddess. In spite of her efforts, she and Angel are drifting closer and closer.

Tess' honest and upright nature is clearly indicated in these two chapters. She is aware of her physical charms, and of her possible usefulness to Angel as a farmer's wife, but she believes that her unfortunate past has made marriage impossible for her. In her mind, she is not good enough for Angel, and she believes she has no real right even to enjoy his company. His honorable nature makes him unlike any man she has ever known. To her, he is truly "angelic" and godlike. As we shall see, she is not far wrong in her innocent estimation. There is much that is not quite human about Angel.

QUESTION: How does the evening sun, "like a great inflamed wound in the sky," symbolize Tess' grief about her past?

CHAPTER 23

Summary

When two months have passed from the time of her arrival at Talbothays, Tess agrees to go with the other dairymaids to church about four miles away. It is a hot July Sunday, but the lanes are muddy and sometimes flooded due to previous thunderstorms. Dressed in their Sunday finery, the girls are dismayed when their path is suddenly blocked by a deep pool of water. Angel Clare, making his rounds to survey storm damage, arrives and offers to carry the girls across the water. He takes Marian first, then Izz, then Retty. Finally it is Tess' turn. Angel murmurs to her, "Three Leahs to get one Rachel," and Tess understands his Biblical allusion. As he lifts her over the pool, he speaks to her tenderly and Tess realizes how very much she loves him. Angel then bids them good-bye, but the emotionally charged situation has not been lost on Tess' friends. Although they are themselves hopelessly in love with Angel, they show no jealousy toward Tess.

That night the other girls are depressed and downcast. They tell Tess that they have heard "a young lady of his own rank" has been chosen for Angel by his family — although "he don't care much for her, they say." This information makes Tess determine to give up any "foolish thought" that Angel might marry her. She assures her friends that she will never take Angel's attentions seriously.

Commentary

Tess' superiority to the other three dairymaids is brought out in this chapter. She is more intelligent and more beautiful than they are, but she sadly reflects that any one of them is more worthy of Angel than she is. She has revelled in his embrace as he carried her across the water, but the futility of loving him is clear to her now, especially since she has learned of the girl his family wants him to marry.

Hardy's understanding of the effect of passion on human beings is shown when he calls the sexual attraction felt for Angel by the three girls "cruel Nature's law." He writes: "The differences which distinguished them as individuals were abstracted by this passion, and each was but portion of one organism called sex." But the girls are realists. They see the social gulf which separates them from Angel. At the same time, they are too generous in spirit to resent Angel's attentions to Tess. Their generosity will work to her advantage in the future.

QUESTION: When Hardy speaks of the love the four girls feel for Angel he says that "there is contagion in this sentiment, . . ." Explain what he means by that remark.

CHAPTER 24

Summary

The "warm ferments" of July are no warmer than "the state of hearts at Talbothays Dairy." Angel feels his growing love for Tess as a burden. Watching her at milking, he is struck by the sweetness, the "humanity" of her features. At last, unable to control his feelings, he takes her by surprise and embraces her. "With unreflecting inevitableness," Tess yields to his embrace, her eyes filling with tears. All her resolutions are useless now. Angel has let "his heart ... outrun his judgment," and he must let Tess know he loves her. The two move apart, but things are no longer the same. Their feelings are out in the open, and neither can ignore them any longer. What one does will now have its impact upon the other, for better or worse.

Commentary

Angel's declaration of love is another of the revealed secrets upon which the plot pivots. It is not surprising that the "heavy scents" and "outward heats" of the summer should have encouraged his natural impulsiveness. But it is rare for him to let his heart rule his head. Tess' response to his embrace gives him good reason to hope, and the influence of burgeoning Nature all about him would have been too much for any "practical man." Nature is not "practical," only creative.

QUESTION: How has the "pivot of the universe" changed for Tess and Angel with Angel's avowal of love?

Phase the Fourth: The Consequence

CHAPTER 25

Summary

That evening Angel is confused, not knowing "what to think of himself." He remembers that he came to the dairy only as a temporary pupil, determined to view the world objectively. But suddenly his feelings have become subjective. He used to believe that what happened to the poor and lowly was not of much consequence (a common notion of the time). Now he realizes that even a milkmaid can possess "a mighty personality." The importance of life now seems to have more to do with experience than environment. A sensitive, intelligent peasant, he realizes, can have a fuller, richer life than a stupid ruler. This new understanding, plus his strong conscience, makes Angel determine not to trifle with Tess and her feelings, but to try to hold aloof from her until he knows whether or not he is ready to ask her to marry him. To gain time to think the matter through, he leaves Talbothays to pay a short visit to his family. His departure causes Tess some pain, for she knows his apprenticeship at Talbothays will soon be over, and she may never see him again.

As he approaches his home, Angel marvels at his feeling for Tess and wonders what his family would say about such a marriage. He passes Mercy Chant, the girl his parents hope he will marry. He rides on, glad she has not seen him.

Upon Angel's arrival at his home, we are introduced to his parents. The Reverend James Clare is an old-fashioned type of clergyman. He is a strong adherent of the doctrines of Luther and Calvin, a believer in the teachings that some souls are predetermined by God for salvation, while others are hopelessly lost. He would have been shocked to know of the "natural life and lush womanhood" at Talbothays. But in spite of his rigid beliefs, the old man has a kind nature and a good heart.

Angel's family notices how free his manners have become. On his part, he is increasingly conscious of how his view of life differs from theirs. Felix and Cuthbert, his brothers, have both entered the clergy. They see Angel as "behaving like a farmer." He sees them as stiff and unobservant, out of touch with life and humanity. At dinner, Angel expects his mother to serve the blackpuddings and mead he has brought as gifts from Mrs. Crick. Instead, she has given the food to some poor parishioners and put the mead into her medicine chest because it is "so extremely alcoholic."

Commentary

The sight of Mercy Chant, a narrow-minded, colorless girl, makes Angel realize how alive and desirable Tess is. Although she might be classed as a "heathen," the comparison of her warmth and vitality with the prim Mercy is in Tess' favor. Angel's family also suffers by contrast. Their unbending "uprightness" contrasts sharply with the way Angel now thinks and feels. Angel (and Hardy) sees their view of religion as lifeless. These anemic souls, Hardy seems to be saying, cannot tolerate the rich life-giving mead and blackpuddings. This chapter emphasizes Hardy's rebellion against organized religion. He points out that "contented dogmatists" like Angel's brothers tend to lose their intellectual grasp as well as their hold on reality.

mead: fermented drink made of honey
tipple: country ale

QUESTION: What does the following statement tell us about the character of Angel's brothers: "When Wordsworth was enthroned they carried pocket copies; and when Shelley was belittled they allowed him to grow dusty on their shelves?"

CHAPTER 26

Summary

Later that day Angel tells his father about his plans. Mr. Clare

41

seems willing to go along with them, and has even set some money aside so that Angel can purchase land. This thoughtfulness encourages Angel to introduce a topic even closer to his heart — Tess. He asks his father what kind of woman would make the best wife for a farmer. "A truly Christian woman," replies James Clare. He is obviously thinking of Mercy Chant. To emphasize Tess' qualifications, Angel tells him he has found a woman who is "chaste as a vessel," with every qualification for a farmer's wife. At this point his mother enters the room, and asks if this girl is "a lady." Angel admits that she is only "a cottager's daughter," but a lady "in feeling and nature." Angel's parents realize he is serious. They raise no strong objections, but only ask him not to marry in haste, and to bring Tess home so that they can meet her. Angel fears their prejudices, but he thinks them less important than Tess' "vital features" — her character and worth.

Mr. Clare rides part of the way with Angel on the return to Talbothays. He admits he is thought too old-fashioned by other clergymen, but says that nevertheless he has converted many sinners — one of them "a young upstart squire named d'Urberville." Angel is touched by his father's story, and feels closer to the old clergyman "on the human side."

Commentary

A sinister note has been introduced — the mention of Alec d'Urberville, whose life has touched that of the Clares and has thus once more moved closer to Tess. The old man tells Angel that Alec insulted and cursed him at their first meeting; this attack on the father will later be repeated on the son, though the two younger men will never meet. In this chapter, James Clare is emerging as a character of more than one dimension. He is not just stuffy and old-fashioned, but a man with feelings and ideals. He has a genuine charity of spirit, and Angel begins to appreciate his father's true goodness.

QUESTION: What means does Angel intend to use to "improve" Tess' religious convictions?

CHAPTER 27

Summary

Arriving at Talbothays, Angel is again struck by the beauty of the valley. Breathing in the "vast pool of odor," he feels as though he had thrown off the "splints and bandages" imposed by his strict family. When he enters the farmhouse, Tess is just coming downstairs, fresh from an afternoon nap. "The brim-fulness of her nature breathed from her." The two embrace, and Tess looks at him "as Eve at her second waking might have regarded Adam." In the milk-house, Angel tells her he wants to marry her. Tess turns "quite careworn," and says that it cannot be. No, she is not engaged to anyone else. She cannot marry, she only wants to love him, she says. Angel patiently tells her that he will give her time to think about it, and distracts her by talking of his family. But when he recounts his father's story of the "young upstart squire," Tess recognizes the description of Alec, and hopelessly remembers "the turmoil of her own past." She again tells Angel that their marriage cannot be, but Angel is determined that it shall be. He has chosen Tess for his wife "from unconstrained Nature, and not from the abodes of Art."

Commentary
The contrast of the valley where Talbothays stands with the austere home of the Clares again strikes Angel, and he sees its lushness of "unconstrained Nature" personified by Tess, "warm as a sunned cat" from her sleep. He is impelled by her beauty to ask her to marry him "without quite meaning to do it so soon." There is again a hint of the Eden they are about to lose. Tess turns to Angel "like Eve," but when she yawns, she somehow reminds him of a serpent.

Evangelical: Contained in or relating to the four Gospels
Tractarian: Supporter of a system of principles set forth in the *Tracts for the Times*, a series of pamphlets issued at Oxford in 1833-4. These tracts were the work of the early leaders of the movement toward Catholicism in the Church of England known as *The Oxford Movement*.
Pantheistic: Believing that God is the combined forces and laws manifested in the existing universe, or worshiping gods of different creeds or cults.

QUESTION: Why do you think Angel has no desire to "disturb" Tess' religious principles?

CHAPTERS 28 AND 29

Summary
Angel is undaunted by Tess' refusal of his proposal. In the days that follow he assures her that his parents won't scorn her for not being a "fine lady." But Tess tells him that she is only refusing him for his own good, even though she loves him dearly. He thinks her reason is that she feels inferior, and tells her that her natural quickness will teach her all she needs to know in order to occupy a higher station in life. He continues to propose, and Tess realizes that "I can't bear to let anybody have him but me! Yet it is wrong to him, and may kill him when he knows." How can she marry Angel without telling him of her past life?

On a Sunday morning, Crick tells the dairyfolk that Jack Dollop has married a widow. Dollop was the young man who wronged his sweetheart, and was beaten inside a churn by her mother (Chapter 21). It seems that he never did marry the girl, preferring to take as a wife a widow with capital. The joke is on Dollop, for his wife's income has stopped with her remarriage. The group discusses whether or not the widow should have told Dollop what would happen to her money. Tess thinks so. Her answer is as much to Angel's proposal as to the matter under discussion: "I think she ought to have told him the true state of things, or else refused him." Once more she has the strength of mind to refuse Angel when he again asks her to marry him.

Undiscouraged, Angel continues to woo her, and Tess knows that she cannot hold out much longer. She again tries to interest him in the other dairymaids, but he has eyes only for her. Tess is glad, and becomes almost resigned to answering Angel's persistent question: "Is it to be yes at last?" One evening in September it becomes necessary for Angel to drive the milk from the dairy to the evening train. He asks Tess to accompany him, and the two drive off together in the wagon.

Commentary

The slow attrition of Tess' resolution is hastened by the fact that the declining summer means the time for Angel's departure is nearing. There is another fateful autumn and winter ahead — another bitter harvest for Tess.

QUESTION: Do you believe Tess should have told Angel of her affair with Alec when he first asked her to marry him?

CHAPTER 30

Summary

Along the way to the railway station, Tess and Angel are "absorbed in the sense of being close to each other." Angel reminds her that she has promised to answer his proposal on this day. They pass the ruins of a manor house which once belonged to the d'Urbervilles, and Angel tells Tess of this extinct Norman family. Tess remains silent until they have reached the railway station and unloaded the milk cans. On the way home, Angel says that it is for his "convenience as well as my happiness" that Tess marry him. She determines then to tell him about herself, beginning with her early life at Marlott. She mentions her d'Urberville ancestry, and Angel is interested because, as he says, "society is hopelessly snobbish" and will think better of her for her d'Urberville blood. He suggests she take the original spelling of her name, but she refuses, saying it would be unlucky. Then he urges that she take his name instead. At last Tess says yes, but bursts into tears, "because I have broken down in my vow! I said I would die unmarried!" Then, kissing Angel passionately, she tells him she loves him, and that she must write to her mother in Marlott. When she mentions "Marlott," Angel realizes where he has seen her before — at the May Day dancing. Tess also recalls that day. She wonders aloud if his not choosing to dance with her then will be an ill omen for them now.

Commentary

In this important chapter, Tess decides to snatch at happiness by marrying Angel. She also begins to tell him about herself — but she omits any mention of Alec. The name of d'Urberville occurs often in their conversation as the couple drive through the countryside, and its sound is ominous to Tess. It is Alec's name as well as her own, and it links them together forever.

Tess seems blissfully unaware that once more, as in Chapter 11, she is riding through the night, close to a man who means to capture her, and to whom she will give herself. Once again summer is ending (as in Chapter 11), and she will again put her trust in someone unwisely.

Notice Hardy's description of the arrival of the train. He sees it as an unwelcome extension of modern mechanized civilization, but this time he does not regard it with his usual fear and loathing. The train is not yet a successful extension. It intrudes, but it is almost swallowed up by the enveloping countryside.

QUESTION: Why is Angel glad to hear of Tess' noble ancestry even though he is supposed to "hate old families"?

CHAPTER 31

Summary

Tess writes to her mother, asking if she should tell Angel about Alec. Mrs. Durbeyfield brusquely tells her not to be a fool. Many women, she writes, have such "bygone troubles," even high-born ladies. But they don't "trumpet" their troubles, so why should Tess? She urges her daughter to marry and keep silent about her affair with Alec, "especially as it is so long ago, and not your fault at all." Tess decides to take her advice, and dismiss the past. She relaxes in Angel's company, and finds him as kind, protective, and chivalrous as she had dreamed.

As is customary in the countryside, the engaged couple are left to each other's company in the October out-of-doors. Tess is "irradiated into forgetfulness of her past sorrows," and oblivious to the fateful (for her) return of autumn. Angel tells her that they may leave England when they are married, and asks her to set a date for the wedding, but at that moment Mr. and Mrs. Crick intrude. Angel tells them of the forthcoming marriage, and Crick warmly praises Tess as "a prize for any man." Later, the girls with whom Tess shares a room wait for her. They are sad for themselves, but glad for her. "You were his choice," they tell her, "and we never hoped to be chosen by him." Tess feels remorseful at their kindness, and resolves to tell Angel the whole truth about herself. It would be better to have him despise her for the truth, she thinks, than to preserve the treachery of silence.

Commentary

Although her mother's letter seemed to shift from Tess' mind the responsibility of telling the truth to Angel, the attitude of her friends brings it back to her. She has indeed been "chosen," and she feels she will be unworthy of Angel's love if she keeps her secret. To her "his soul is the soul of a saint, his intellect that of a seer." But will she lose him if she tells him? That is the question that racks her now.

The insights given into Angel's character in this chapter will help us to understand his later actions. He is idealistic: "rather bright than hot." There is more of the spiritual and intellectual in his nature than the physical, and Hardy tells us his love for Tess is "imaginative and ethereal." He plans to teach her and turn her into a lady worthy of his mother's regard, and is proud that she has caught "his manners and habits, his speeches and phrases . . ."

For the first time, Tess is happy — even though she is aware of "those shapes of darkness" in the background. Her secret past seems to be "approaching" a little nearer every day. Wistfully, she longs to save herself by turning back the clock. "Why didn't you stay and love me when I was sixteen, living with my little sisters and brothers, and you danced on the green?" she cries to Angel. But she cannot tell him why there is so much bitterness and regret in her voice.

baily: an officer whose duty it is to collect taxes; a bailiff; a district under a bailiff

QUESTION: Why does Hardy describe Angel as being "less Byronic than Shelleyan?"

CHAPTER 32

Summary

Tess continues to delay her confession. She wishes she could remain engaged — "a perpetual betrothal" — and thus postpone the inevitable forever. With the oncoming winter, there is less work for the dairymaids. Crick suggests to Angel that he take Tess with him when he leaves Talbothays at Christmastime. Angel urges Tess to name a wedding day, and she reluctantly fixes the date as December 31st. She again writes her mother for advice, but Mrs. Durbeyfield does not reply.

Events seem to whirl Tess on. Angel's plans are vague — it may be a year or two before he begins farming — and Tess timidly suggests postponing the wedding until he is settled. But he is not anxious to have her out of his sight because her speech and manners are improving steadily under his influence. He hopes she will soon be poised enough to be introduced to his mother. Meanwhile, he has been offered an opportunity to learn the operation of a flour mill. He is moved to accept the offer because the mill is on the estate formerly owned by the d'Urbervilles. He decides that he and Tess will spend their honeymoon there. When Tess discovers that the banns for the marriage have not been called in church, Angel explains that they will be married privately by licence. Tess is relieved that no one who knows her history will hear of the banns and object to the marriage, but she is also uneasy. Perhaps she will be punished by God if the banns are not called. When Angel buys her a trousseau and a wedding dress, she wonders if the dress will betray her past by changing color — as was the case in an old ballad her mother used to sing.

Commentary

The lack of banns is another ominous note that clouds the forth-coming wedding, and Angel's secrecy about the wedding reflects hidden doubts on his part about Tess' suitability as his wife. The choice of New Year's Eve as a wedding date is symbolic, for with the wedding Tess' happiness will end. She will begin her new life in a fateful lodging — a building that was once part of the d'Urberville estate. Tess' associations with her ancient name have always been disastrous.

QUESTION: In what ways is Tess contributing to her own down-fall?

CHAPTER 33

Summary

On Christmas Eve, Angel takes Tess shopping in a nearby town. While Tess waits for Angel to bring a horse and carriage to the inn where they have put up, she stands in the entrance. Two men pass her. One remarks on her beauty, but the other questions her virtue, and Tess recognizes him as a man from Trantridge. Angel overhears his remark and knocks him down, forcing him to apologize. Shaken by the scene, Tess urges Angel to postpone the wedding, but he refuses. That night at Talbothays, Tess hears the sounds of a struggle from Angel's room. She investigates, and discovers that Angel has been thrashing about in the throes of a dream about the fight with the Trantridge man. She returns to her room and writes Angel a full confession of her affair with Alec. She puts it into an envelope and slips it under his door.

The next morning he makes no mention of the confession, greeting her with his usual kiss. Tess cannot understand. She wonders if he read her letter, or whether he has forgiven her so easily. The wedding day arrives, but no one has been invited from Marlott. Angel's parents have written a rather cold letter, and Angel feels they have responded this way because they think he is marrying beneath him. Angel is not disturbed at this, as he plans to present Tess to them "as a d'Urberville and a lady," once she has travelled with him for a time and benefited from his tutoring.

47

in a funeral procession." Tess continually begs for mercy, saying that she was "a child when it happened. I knew nothing of men." He admits that she was "more sinned against than sinning," but does not seem to love her any longer. She offers to drown herself in the nearby river, but he orders her back to the house. She lies down in her room, where she falls into a miserable sleep.

When Angel returns, he looks in on her. He feels pity and a sudden tenderness for her, but the sight of the d'Urberville portraits makes him turn away from her door and go downstairs with a "sterile expression" on his face.

Commentary

Tess has revealed herself to Angel, and he has revealed himself to us. He is no godlike being, but a weak and cold-hearted man with a "small, compressed mouth." His rebellion against the teachings of his family seems swallowed up by the traditional moral attitudes he once scorned. Like his brothers, he now judges Tess by appearances. She is no longer the splendid "child of nature" in his eyes, but only the weak remnant of a corrupt line. He bitterly regrets having married her instead of a woman of money and position.

Even in this personal tragedy, Hardy offers us his view of the indifference of Fate and Nature to human misery. He writes:

> The night came in, and took up its place there, unconcerned and indifferent; the night which had already swallowed up his happiness, and was now digesting it listlessly; and was ready to swallow up the happiness of a thousand other people with as little disturbance or change of mien.

QUESTION: Why do you think the sight of the d'Urberville portraits makes Angel decide not to comfort Tess?

CHAPTER 36

Summary

When Angel awakes the next morning, he begs Tess to tell him that her confession is not true: she looks so fresh and pure that he finds her story incredible. She cannot deny it. He asks her if her seducer is still alive and in England, and again she must answer yes. Tess tells him that he has "lost all around," and begs him to divorce her. Angel tells her this is impossible — the publicity, expense, and difficulty of divorce rule it out. She then says that she thought of hanging herself last night, and the shocked Angel makes her promise she will never attempt such a thing. The morning passes in misery. Angel goes off to the mill, determined to pursue his education in farming. He returns for meals, but Tess knows she has not won him back. A few days later, he tells her he can no longer live with her without despising himself. If Alec were dead, he remarks, they might have a chance at happiness. A separation seems the only solution for the time being. Tess offers to begin it by going home, and Angel agrees. "I think of people more kindly when I am away from them," he tells her.

Commentary

Tess' meek acceptance of whatever Angel says or does is in startling contrast to her fiery reaction to Alec. With Angel, she seems always in the position of a worshipper. "She took everything as her deserts," Hardy writes. "A woman of the world might have conquered him." But Tess is only a simple country girl, with the real Tess before him, Angel can no longer imagine her as his pure ideal.

It is Angel who seems to have within his gentle nature a "hard logical deposit, like a vein of metal in soft loam," but it is Tess who has the strength to make the break. Her reasons would touch the stoniest heart. If they stay together, she tells him, he might someday "be tempted to say words, and they might be overheard, perhaps by my own children. O, what only hurts me now would torture and kill me then!"

QUESTION: Why does Tess declare that suicide "is too good for me, after all?"

CHAPTERS 37 AND 38

Summary

That night Angel again walks in his sleep, as he did at Talbothays. He enters Tess' room, murmuring, "Dead, dead, dead." He wraps her in a sheet, as in a shroud, and lifts her from her bed "with as much respect as one would show to a dead body." Then he carries her from the house to the grounds of a ruined abbey, where he places her in an empty stone coffin. On the way to the abbey, he carries her across the river, and Tess thinks he must be reliving the day when he carried her through the flood near Talbothays (Chapter 23). Realizing that Angel is still asleep, Tess leads him back to his bed in the cottage.

He does not appear to remember anything of the night's happening in the morning. He has ordered a carriage, and they leave the cottage. On the way they stop at Talbothays, keeping their estrangement secret, although Tess finds it hard to conceal her unhappiness. When the visit is over, they go on to the crossroads near Marlott, and there they part. Angel tells her "there is no anger between us," but she must not come to him until he comes to her, "if I can bring myself to bear it." He gives her some money and takes the jewels for safekeeping in a bank. They go their separate ways.

When Tess reaches Marlott, one of the villagers tells her that her father is celebrating her marriage at the Pure Drop Inn. Sick at heart, Tess cannot face a public homecoming, and she chooses a back path to her home. Once there, she tells her mother all that has happened. Joan Durbeyfield calls her a fool, and then murmurs in resignation that "what's done can't be undone." Tess' father, however, takes the news badly. His concern is what his cronies will say to him now about Tess' "mighty match." Tess realizes that she cannot remain at Marlott. When a letter comes from Angel, she tells her parents that she is going to join him in northern England. She gives half her money to her mother "as a slight return for all the trouble and humiliation" she has brought upon the family. As Tess hoped, her parents now believe all is well with the young couple.

Commentary

The lurid and unconvincing sleepwalking scene makes a strong point. Unconsciously, Angel wishes Tess were dead so that he could part from her forever without causing her pain. Once awake, however, he is motivated only by that "hard, logical deposit" in his rational mind. His intellect rules his emotions, and makes it possible for him to be so unfeeling toward Tess. Notice that the seasonal changes at Talbothays reflect Tess' own despair: "The gold of the summer picture was now gray, the colours mean, the rich soil mud, and the river cold."

Jack Durbeyfield, whom even his wife calls a "poor, silly man," again proves himself an unstable reed that his daughter cannot hope to lean on. As always, he is more concerned with the opinions of his drinking companions than with his family's misery. It is ironic that Mrs. Durbeyfield should say, "I'm sure I don't know why children o' my bringing forth should all be bigger simpletons than other people's." The wonder is that her daughter should be a person of such intelligence and integrity. When Tess discovers that her bed "had been adapted for two younger children," she knows she no longer has a place at home. The giving up of half of her money is an unusual bit of face-saving for the honest, direct Tess. She wants her parents to think that "the wife of Angel Clare could well afford it."

QUESTION: Why does Hardy seem to feel it would have been better for Tess to have staged an emotional scene when parting from Angel?

CHAPTER 39

Summary

Like Tess, Angel must try to save face with his parents. He now believes that all his troubles stem from the "accident of her being a d'Urberville." He should have stuck to his policy of despising old families, for then he would not now have to reconstruct his life without Tess. On his travels toward home, he notices posters advertising farm land for sale cheaply in Brazil to "emigrating agriculturists." Perhaps, he thinks, he might make a new life in Brazil. Perhaps in time Tess might join him there, and in that "country of contrasting scenes and notions," Tess' error might be forgotten.

When he tells his family of his plans to emigrate, he does not let them know of his estrangement from Tess. His parents think she is merely visiting her family. Angel is cross-examined by his mother about Tess' appearance and moral character, and seems satisfied with his answers, but when his father reads the chapter in Proverbs praising a virtuous wife, Angel becomes so upset that his mother knows something is wrong. He admits that he and Tess have "had a difference." When his mother demands to know whether Tess' history will bear investigation, Angel declares, "She is spotless" — determined to lie even if it damns him. Satisfied, his mother leaves him. Angel is left with the knowledge that he is, after all, a slave to convention who has allowed his wrecked marriage to wreck his hopes of a career.

Commentary

Angel's reaction to Tess' confession has shattered all his "attempted independence of judgment." He is no longer a rebel, but has fallen back into his family's prudish ways of thinking. He only regrets his lost career because it would have been respectable enough to suit his father and brothers. He blames his wife for his own failure, but has not the perception to see that Tess, like the woman of the proverb, is a virtuous wife whose "price is above rubies." Angel's ability to rationalize is his "fatal flaw." It brings both him and Tess to disaster.

QUESTION: Since the wedding, Hardy has ceased to refer to Angel Clare as "Angel." He now calls him "Clare." Explain this change.

CHAPTER 40

Summary

While winding up his affairs before going to Brazil, Angel meets Mercy Chant in town. As always, her narrow-minded prejudices repel him, and he tries to shock her. He pays into the bank another 30 pounds to be sent to Tess. Angel believes this sum will see her through, especially as he has told her to get in touch with his father in case of an emergency, but he does not make it possible for his family to communicate with Tess because they might find out about the estrangement.

Before leaving England, he goes back to the house at Wellbridge to pay the rent and return the key. Everything there reminds him of Tess, and he wonders for the first time if he was wise to leave her. He meets Izz, Tess' friend from Talbothays, and tells her of the separation. He can never live with Tess again, he says, and he may never be able to love anyone else. At Angel's prodding, Izz confesses her love for him. In a sudden overthrowing of convention, he asks her to come with him to

Brazil, but withdraws the offer just as suddenly when she tells him Tess would have died for him. He realizes now how good Tess is, but he does not try to return to her. If he was right at first, he must be right now. The facts have not changed. Five days later, Angel leaves for Brazil.

Commentary

Hardy uses the reappearance of Mercy Chant to bring out his own feeling about persons who profess to be religious. He has her say, "I glory in my Protestanism," and then shows the reader how inglorious her small-mindedness is.

As always, Angel's attempts to break the rules of convention bring misery to others — this time to poor Izz. By impulsively giving in to a whim of the moment, he gives her wild hope and then dashes it.

Although Izz gives Angel new insight into Tess, he does not go back to her. He is determined to stick to his "principles," and thus becomes as uncharitable as Mercy.

QUESTION: When they part why does Angel tell Izz he can never forget her?

CHAPTERS 41 AND 42

Summary

Eight months after Tess and Angel have separated, Tess' money is almost gone. She has worked at dairy farms and as a harvest field hand, but after that bad weather forced her to live off most of the money that remained. Her mother writes, asking for 20 pounds to repair the cottage roof, and Tess sends her all but 10 pounds of the money Angel had banked for her before leaving for Brazil. Almost destitute in the face of the coming winter, Tess is still reluctant to ask Angel's parents for help.

Meanwhile, Angel lies ill of fever in Brazil. Like the other Englishmen who came there to farm, he has lost his crops and ruined his health. Unaware of his troubles, Tess finds work hard to get. A letter from Marian tells her of work to be had on an upland farm, and she sets off on foot.

Tess has lost hope of being reunited with Angel, and she is hoping to "disconnect herself ... from her eventful past." But she cannot disconnect herself from her distinctive beauty. It attracts the unwelcome attention of the man from Trantridge who fought with Angel the previous Christmas. Frightened, Tess runs from him into the woods, and sleeps fitfully under the trees. When she awakens she finds a number of dying birds, shot by hunters, and she feels ashamed when she contrasts their misery with her own.

After making sure no one is lurking on the highway, Tess resumes her journey. She dons her oldest clothes to foil the admiring glances of young men in the towns along the way, cuts off her eyebrows, and ties a handkerchief around her face as if she had a toothache. Her disguise is so successful that the next man she meets calls her a scarecrow: she truly appears to be a field-woman, "with no sign of young passion in her."

The farm proves to be located near the upland village of Flint-comb-Ash, a desolate place with poor soil. Tess finds Marian, and each woman is struck by the other's altered appearance. "But you *be* a gentleman's wife," says Marian, "and it seems hardly fair that you should live like this!" Tess begs her to ask no questions about Angel, and not to call her "Mrs. Clare."

As Marian says, Flintcomb-Ash is a "starve-acre place," fit only to grow wheat and turnips. The work there is back-breaking, and the pay low. Tess signs on as a field laborer, agreeing to stay until Old Lady-Day (April 6). She writes her parents to give them her address, but tells them nothing "of the sorriness of her situation; it might have brought reproach upon him [Angel]."

Commentary

Another fatal autumn and winter have overtaken Tess. Again she is abandoned. She does not think of finding work in town where her intelligence and willingness would have been appreciated. Like her friends, she knows only agricultural work and fears "non-rural gentility." But, as always, her beauty makes her a target; she is not safe in her native countryside. Like the pheasants, she is hunted into the woods.

Although she has no hope, she continues to go through the motions of living, willingly enduring "injustice, punishment . . . execution."

Flintcomb-Ash, a place "almost sublime in its dreariness," is symbolically located on a plateau lying "between the valley of her birth and the valley of her love." (Note the aptness of its name — hard as flint, dry as ashes.) Here she has come to endure her punishment. For once she has a faithful friend to help her. Marian, like Tess, has also lost Angel.

Cybele: Nature goddess of ancient peoples of Anatolia
corn and potatoes: Hardy probably meant wheat and turnips
swede-hacking: weeding and harvesting turnips
lanchets (or lynchets): unplowed and untilled strips of land
thirtover: thwarting or obstructing

QUESTION: Do you agree with Marian that Tess' plight is the fault of "something outside them both?"

CHAPTER 43

Summary

Hardy tells us a good deal about Flintcomb-Ash with the words, "The single fat thing on the soil was Marian herself; and she was an importation." She and Tess work in the turnip fields no matter what the weather. The only solace the two girls can find is in talking of the happy days at Talbothays, "that tract of land where summer had been liberal in her gifts. . . ."

Hoping to brighten their lot, Marian writes to Izz and asks her to join them at Flintcomb-Ash. It is winter when Izz arrives; it is terribly cold and the field work is halted. Until the weather changes, the women work in the barn pulling straw from sheaves of wheat. Tess sees another familiar — but unwelcome — face when she meets her employer in the barn. He is the man from Trantridge, the man who fought with Angel and who later annoyed her on the road. He tells her that "now I think I've got the better of you," and demands that she beg his pardon for the beating given him by Angel. Tess refuses. He then tells her she must work longer hours than the rest in order to match the production quota of the more experienced workers.

When the older workers leave in the afternoon, Tess remains in the barn. Marian and Izz stay on to help her. When Tess collapses from the heavy work, her employer enters and demands that she stand up and finish the task. Finally, even Izz finds the "reed drawing" too exhausting, and she leaves. Alone with Tess, Marian (made confiding by the bottle she always has with her) tells Tess about Angel's offer to take Izz to Brazil with him. Tess is upset by this news, though it makes her realize how negligent she has been about writing to Angel. But when she begins her letter, she stops, wondering "how could she write entreaties to him, or show that she cared for him any more," when he had proposed to run off with Izz.

Commentary

Nothing could present a greater contrast to the lushness of Talbothays than this bleak intolerable landscape. Even in this bleak misery, Tess and Marian are able to take comfort in their memories of "green, sunny, romantic Talbothays." This is a classic example of Hardy's premise that "two forces were at work here as everywhere, the inherent will to enjoy, and the circumstantial will against enjoyment."

Through a rather labored coincidence, Tess' employer turns out to be Groby, the man who has on two occasions persecuted her. He takes no advantage of his position, strangely enough, beyond making her working conditions more difficult. Tess prefers his abuse to his "gallantry."

QUESTION: Is Tess' resentment of Angel for asking Izz to go away with him in character? Would you have expected her to accept this news with her usual humility and docility?

CHAPTER 44

Summary

Although Tess cannot bring herself to write Angel, she wonders why she has not heard from him. Stung by Izz's story, she assumes he is indifferent to her. But perhaps he is ill? She summons "the courage of solicitude" to call at the home of Angel's parents for news.

Dressed in her best clothes, carrying her best shoes, she sets out to walk the fifteen miles to Emminster on a Sunday morning. She hopes "to win the heart of her mother-in-law," and "gain back the truant [Angel]." No one answers when she rings the bell at the vicarage, and she realizes the family has gone to church. She goes to the churchyard gate to wait, and is soon caught up in the crowd leaving the church. The stares of the townsfolk make her uncomfortable, and she walks ahead to wait until lunch time is past. Hearing voices behind her, Tess recognizes the similarity of the tones of the two men speaking to Angel's voice. She realizes they are Angel's brothers.

Ahead of them walks a young woman. Tess hears one of the brothers say, "There is Mercy Chant. Let us overtake her." This, she knows, must be the young woman Angel's parents chose for him. Her heart sinks when she hears one of the Clare brothers sigh, "I never see that nice girl [Mercy] without more and more regretting his precipitancy in throwing himself away on a dairymaid ..." One of the brothers notices the boots Tess has hidden in the bushes when she changed to her best shoes. Mercy also sees them, and takes them with her to give "to some poor person."

Sure that the Clare family has only contempt for her, Tess leaves Emminster. She does not know that her present condition "was precisely one which would have enlisted the sympathies of old Mr. and Mrs. Clare."

Wearing her thin shoes, Tess walks back toward Flintcomb-Ash. Along the way she stops for refreshment, and is told by the woman who serves her that everyone in the neighborhood is listening to a preacher. Curious, Tess listens outside the barn where he is speaking. She hears the preacher refer to himself as "the greatest of sinners," who has been reformed by an elderly clergyman who bore his insults with prayer and charity. Tess suddenly recognizes the speaker's voice as that of Alec d'Urberville. She looks in through the barn door — and is face to face with her seducer.

Commentary

"The greatest misfortune of her life" is the way Hardy describes Tess' failure to see Angel's parents. Had she done so, her story might have ended happily. But she judged Mr. and Mrs. Clare by their supercilious sons, and let pride rather than instinct guide her. In Hardy's view, disaster must follow when we avoid what is natural and regulate our actions by pride or vanity. Mr. Clare's genuine kindness would have led him to help Tess, but she has the bad luck to judge him by his sons, who possess little compassion. Mercy's appropriation of Tess' boots is particularly ironic. Tess has lost everything she values, and Mercy's "charity" now deprives her of the comfort of stout footwear. So it is that Tess turns from a confrontation that would have saved her to one with Alec which dooms her.

QUESTION: Why would Angel's parents have looked upon Tess as a worthy person to love?

Phase the Sixth: The Convert

CHAPTER 45

Summary

Even though Alec publicly claims to be a "converted man, sorrowing for his past irregularities," Tess feels a great fear of him. He now wears a "version of minister's clothing, and his expression is pious and supplicating." Tess feels this state of affairs is unnatural, and Hardy cynically writes, "Animalism had become fanaticism."

Before she can get away, Alec sees and recognizes her. The sight of her is an equal shock to him. He overtakes her on the road to Flintcomb-Ash and tells her that he wants to try and "save" her — "the woman I had so grievously wronged." He explains that heaven and the action of the Reverend James Clare (who converted him) have saved him. Tess rebukes him for taking his "fill of pleasure on earth" and then trying to secure salvation by being converted. She does not believe in his idea of religion because, she tells him, a better man [Angel] does not. Nor does she believe Alec's conversion will be permanent. Alec, however, appears to be sincere. He asks her to veil her face so her beauty will not disturb him. They walk on until they reach a forlorn place called "Cross-in-Hand" where a stone pillar stands. Accounts of the history of the pillar differ, but there is "something sinister or solemn" about it.

Tess tells Alec about the baby, and he is "struck mute" with shock. Why did she never let him know? She tells him they cannot meet again and that he must not come near her. He then asks her to swear on the stone pillar that she will never again "tempt me by your charms or ways." Frightened, she does so, and Alec leaves her. When she later meets a shepherd, she asks him about the stone pillar. It is a place of ill-omen, he tells her, and she feels a chill of apprehension.

Commentary

Alec, signifying Tess' "implacable past," overtakes her again. His conversion is not strongly rooted, and Tess unthinkingly weakens it by questioning his beliefs. Thus, she will become "the innocent means of [Alec's] backsliding." It is ironic that Alec should turn for help and comfort to the words of Mr. Clare, the one man who could have helped Tess. The oath Alec makes Tess swear will not help either of them, for it is sworn at an unholy place. By so swearing, Tess may be said to have taken up her own "cross," to carry until her death.

Cyprian: pertaining to the worship of Aphrodite; licentious
petite mort: a "little death." In this case, a chill of foreboding

QUESTION: What does Hardy mean by "Animalism had become fanaticism?"

CHAPTER 46

Summary

Several days later, the "joyless monotony" of Tess' field work is broken by the appearance of Alec. He takes the full responsibility for her ill fortune. "The whole blame was mine," he says of their affair at Trantridge. He offers to make amends by selling the estate left to him by his mother and taking Tess with him to do missionary work in Africa. Tess refuses, telling him she is married. He is surprised and disappointed at this news — "what sort of husband can he be" to leave her in such circumstances? Tess will not tell him Angel's name and begs him to leave, but when he does, she wonders if she would agree to marry Alec if she were free. She decides she would not, for she does not really like him. That night she again tries to write Angel, but does not send the letter.

On Candlemas Eve (the second of February), the laborers prepare to go to Candlemas Fair, where new working contracts for the next year are made. Tess stays at Flintcomb-Ash, but her quietude is interrupted by another visit from Alec. This time, however, he is more like the "old" Alec than the "new." He tells her that he cannot forget her, and asks her to pray for him. "How can I," Tess demands, "when I am forbidden to believe that the great Power who moves the world would alter His plans on my account?" She tells Alec some of Angel's arguments on religion, and weakens his conversion still further. Her unsettling effect on him has made him miss an engagement to preach. "I thought I worshipped in the mountains, but I find I still serve in the groves," he tells her, meaning that his desire for her is stronger than his desire for salvation. Horrified, Tess sees that she has unwittingly turned Alec away from his conversion. She implores him to go, although he insists that he wants only "the legal right to protect you." When he departs, "His eyes were equally barren of worldly and religious faith." All Alec has left is his passion for Tess.

Commentary

It is bitterly ironic that Angel's logic manages to topple Alec's faith. By repeating her husband's arguments to Alec, Tess has removed the only barrier he respected — his new-found religion. Her instinct, which makes her prefer Groby's bullying to Alec's company, is correct. Alec, who wants now to be her defender, can never be anything but her assailant. Although he calls her a "temptress," he recognizes her essential purity, "unsmirched in spite of all." It is sad that Angel, the "good man" whose honor Tess so stoutly defends, is unable to recognize Tess' innocence.

QUESTION: Why does Alec feel responsible for Tess' present state?

CHAPTERS 47 AND 48

Summary

When Alec appears at the farm again, he is no longer dressed as a preacher. Tess is eating her lunch, and she asks him why he continues to bother her. He replies, "You haunt me. . . . The religious channel is left dry forthwith; and it is you who have done it!" Since it is her fault, he continues, she should come away with him. He quotes the words of the prophet Hosea to her: "And she shall follow after her lover, but she shall not overtake him; and she shall seek him, but shall not find him; then shall she say, I will go and return to my first husband; for then it was better with me than now." Tess' only response is to strike him across the face with her heavy leather glove. "I was your master once!" Alec tells her, "I will be your master again. If you are any man's wife, you are mine!" He leaves, but warns that he will return for his answer.

He reappears that afternoon, before the threshing is over. Tess works doggedly on until the rick has been lowered. Groby tells her she may join her "friend" if she likes, but she refuses. Finally the work is done, and Alec insists on walking her home. He tells her that he will provide for her family, "if you will only show confidence in me." The thought of her family sways Tess, but she stiffens her will. "I will take nothing from you, either for them or for me."

In her quarters, she at once writes to Angel. He must come back to her, or let her come to him, she writes. She has been tempted, and "pressed to do what I will not do. . . . come to me, and save me from what threatens me!"

Commentary

If there is anything that Hardy despises as much as hypocritical religious concepts, it is the machine age. Notice that he refers to the threshing machine as a "despot" and "tyrant."

Alec's complex character is explored more fully. He tells Tess he wants to take care of her as her "true husband." He sincerely seems to pity her, yet he is as determined as ever to master her. He blames her for tempting him away from his faith, but he seems relieved that the restrictions of the ministry have fallen away from him. "I'm awfully glad you have made an apostate of me," he tells her. In his opinion, if there is no God, there is no one to struggle to be good for.

Tess seems to be resigned to the role in which life has cast her. "Once victim, always victim — that's the law!" she declares hopelessly. Hardy compares her to a sparrow about to have its neck wrung (he often compares her to a trapped bird), but there is a strength about her that makes her more like an animal at bay. She seems to weaken when Alec tells her he will care for her family, but for once she overcomes her almost sacrificial attitude toward them. "Perhaps you are a little better and kinder than I have been thinking you were," she says, but she trusts neither him nor herself. The letter she writes Angel is desperate.

rick: stack of hay, corn, etc.; often built and thatched
mammet: light meal or picnic

QUESTION: What effect does Alec claim the news of the baby has had upon him?

CHAPTERS 49 AND 50

Summary

Tess sends her desperate letter to the vicarage, and Mr. Clare forwards it to Angel. The Clares are expecting him to leave Brazil for home on the following month, and they hope Tess' letter will speed him on his way. In a rare outburst, Mrs. Clare blames her husband for Angel's misfortunes. "You should have sent him to Cambridge in spite of his want of faith!" Her husband disagrees, but he is nevertheless full of self-reproach. Both are suspicious of Angel's separation from Tess, and blame themselves for "this unlucky marriage."

Meanwhile, Angel is travelling toward the Brazilian coast. He is still suffering the effects of illness, and he has aged mentally (as well as physically) a dozen years. His new maturity has given him insight into morality and Tess' true character. He confides the story of his marriage to another Englishman who tells him he was wrong to leave his wife. Angel agrees with shame and remorse. "Thus from being her critic he grew to be her advocate."

At Flintcomb-Ash, Tess is startled by the arrival of her sister, 'Liza-Lu, who brings news that Mrs. Durbeyfield is very ill. Tess leaves for Marlott at once. At Marlott she nurses her mother and cares for the family. As usual, her father is busy with another fanciful "scheme for living." While he indulges his fancy, Tess tends to more practical matters, such as working on the family plot just outside the village.

One evening, while working by the light of bonfires used to burn grasses, she discovers a man working beside her. He is dressed like a farmer, but she discovers that he is Alec, come to "tempt" her as Satan did Eve — as he puts it. Again he offers to help her family, and again she refuses. "The more fool you!" Alec tells her angrily and leaves.

As Tess nears her home, 'Lisa-Lu comes to tell her that Mr. Durbeyfield has died of a heart attack. Tess knows this means the family is homeless. During her father's life, the house was theirs under a lease that would end with his death. The tenant farmer who owns the house wants it for his own laborers.

Commentary

The thing that Tess has hoped for has happened — Angel loves her again and is coming back to her. But he will arrive too late. Alec has reappeared to Tess, appearing out of the bonfire's smoke and flames like Satan himself — and the temptation of security he offers Tess' family is a strong one in the light of her father's death.

Durbeyfield's death adds to her burdens. As a "lifeholder," he held a lease on his property that ran for the lifetimes of three successive tenants before reverting back to the tenant-farmer owner. Durbeyfield was the third and final tenant. Such lifehold leases were common in the 19th century. Hardy sees a certain poetic justice in the family's loss of their dwelling place. Their ancestors, the knightly d'Urbervilles, had doubtless confiscated many dwellings and turned out their rightful owners. It was now the Durbeyfields' turn to be evicted, a natural part of Hardy's "flux and reflux — the rhythm of chance . . ."

QUESTION: How have Angel's experiences in Brazil affected his mental outlook?

CHAPTERS 51 AND 52

Summary

On the eve of Old Lady-Day, there is an air of "agricultural unrest" in the area around Marlott. Laborers are changing to new farms and new jobs. The village population grows smaller year by year as many of the craftsmen — like Tess' father — lose their homes and migrate to the cities to find jobs. Thus, the villages lose those who had been the holders of their traditions.

The Durbeyfields are among the dispossessed. While Mrs. Durbeyfield pays farewell calls to her friends, Tess sits at home. Alec d'Urberville appears at her window, riding a horse. He tells her the story of the d'Urberville coach — "it is held to be of ill-omen to one who hears it." It seems that one of Tess' ancestors tried to abduct a beautiful woman in the coach, and in the struggle he killed her — or perhaps she killed him: Alec cannot remember which.

Tess tells Alec they are going to Kingsbere, where they have taken rooms. There Mrs. Durbeyfield can be near the "home" of her husband's illustrious ancestors. There Tess can wait for Angel. Alec insists that Angel will never return and offers to shelter the family at Trantridge: "I owe you something for the past, you know. I am glad of the opportunity of repaying you a little." Tess gives him no hope, and he rides away.

Left alone, Tess begins to realize for the first time how badly Angel has treated her. She writes a short note telling Angel she can never forgive him for his cruelty and mails it.

The next morning the Durbeyfields load their household goods on a wagon and leave Marlott. On the way to Kingsbere, Tess meets Marian and Izz, who have left Flintcomb-Ash. Marian tells Tess that "the gentleman who follows 'ee" had come asking for her. "He found me," Tess replies briefly, and admits that Angel has not yet done so. They exchange addresses and part.

At Kingsbere, they learn that Joan's letter to reserve rooms arrived too late; no rooms are free. The family looks for other lodging, but none is to be had. At last Mrs. Durbeyfield has their luggage put down near the old d'Urberville estate. "Isn't your family vault your own freehold?" she demands, and there the family camps. When Mrs. Durbeyfield goes off into town to get food, Tess is left with the little ones.

In the town, Tess' mother meets Alec. She tells him where Tess is, rather unwillingly. Meanwhile, Tess has wandered into the old church on the estate, and for the first time she sees the defaced and broken tombs of her ancestors. Near an old altar-tomb, Alec jumps out at her. Shocked and frightened, she almost faints. He tells her that "the little finger of the sham d'Urberville can do more for you" than all her extinct ancestors. But she only tells him to go away. "Mind you," he says as he leaves, "you'll be civil yet." Alone, Tess looks at the entrance to the vaults, saying, "Why am I on the wrong side of this door!"

Unknown to Tess, Marian and Izz decide to write Angel and tell him that Tess is in danger. They send their letter to the vicarage.

Commentary

Hardy gives a harsh picture of the way artisans are forced out of the villages by farmer landlords. "Cottagers who were not directly employed on the land were looked upon with disfavor, and the banishment of some starved the trade of others, who were thus obliged to follow . . . them to the city where work might be had." He speaks of the so-called "tendency of the rural population toward large towns" (a statistician's concept) as being like "the tendency of water to flow up-hill when forced by machinery."

In stretching out in the tomb, Alec is literally resting upon the d'Urbervilles' past glory. His motive may be base, but his actions do him credit as he continues to try to help Tess and her family. It is hard to dislike Alec entirely in these chapters. His attentions irritate Tess, but drive her to look realistically at Angel's treatment of her.

QUESTION: Who do you feel has wronged Tess the most, Alec or Angel? Why?

Phase the Seventh: Fulfilment

CHAPTER 53

Summary

When Angel arrives at Emminster Vicarage, the Clares are shocked by his appearance, "so reduced was that figure from its former contours by worry." He reads Tess' note telling him she can never forgive him. When his mother tells him not to worry about "a mere child of the soil," Angel indignantly says that Tess is a descendent of "one of the oldest Norman houses." The next day he is ill, and, worrying about how Tess will receive him, he writes to her at Marlott. He receives a reply from Joan Durbeyfield. Tess is away at present, she writes, "I do not feel at liberty to tell you where . . . ." Angel feels rebuked, but when he receives word of Tess' return, he decides he must find her. He asks his father if Tess ever requested money. On being told that she did not, he understands for the first time how much she must have suffered. He tells his parents the facts of his separation, and their sympathy goes out to Tess. As he packs to leave, the letter comes from Marian and Izz.

Commentary

The change the Clares observe in Angel is not merely physical. The "light in his eyes has waned," but so has his sense of self-righteousness. The reader may hope that Angel's new-found wisdom will save Tess, but the days that slip by between his arrival home and his actual search for Tess will constitute a fatal delay. Again we have evidence of the essential goodness and sympathy of his parents, in spite of the uncharitable remark by Mrs. Clare about the "mere child of the soil."

QUESTION: Why does Mrs. Clare change her opinion of Tess after hearing the true facts of the separation?

CHAPTERS 54, 55 AND 56

Summary

Angel drives to Flintcomb-Ash, passing Cross-in-Hand on the way, where Alec compelled Tess to swear she would never "wilfully" tempt him. At Flintcomb-Ash, he understands how hard life has been for Tess. He goes on to Marlott, only to find the Durbeyfield cottage occupied by new tenants. He visits the field where he first saw Tess dancing, and also the churchyard where John Durbeyfield lies beneath a tombstone engraved "HOW ARE THE MIGHTY FALLEN." A sexton tells him that Tess' father wanted to be buried at Kingsbere, but lack of money prevented this. The family has not even been able to pay for the tombstone, so Angel does so before going on to Kingsbere.

In Kingsbere, he finds Tess' mother, who is now "fairly well-provided for." She is unwilling to tell him of her daughter's whereabouts, but finally says Tess has gone to the seaside resort of Sandbourne.

When Angel reaches Sandbourne, it is too late to continue his search. He finds it hard to imagine what a simple country girl can be doing in this fashionable, glittering place. The next morning he goes to the post office, and asks for the address of either "Mrs. Clare" or "Mrs. Durbeyfield." Neither name is listed, but a passerby suggests that he may mean Mrs. d'Urberville, who is staying at The Herons, an elegant lodging.

Angel wonders if Tess may be working at The Herons as a maid. He is unprepared to discover that Mrs. d'Urberville is indeed Tess, but a fashionable, beautifully gowned and groomed Tess he has never before beheld. "Can you forgive me for going away?" he asks her. "Can't you — come to me? How do you get to be — like this?"

Tess, her eyes "shining unnaturally," her voice hard, tells him, "It is too late . . . I waited and waited for you, but you did not come." It is indeed too late, for now she belongs to Alec d'Urberville. "He was very kind to me. . . . He has won me back to him. . . . I didn't care what he did wi' me." But she now hates Alec for telling her that Angel would never come back — "and you have come!"

The confrontation ends. Angel goes, looking "colder and more shrunken." Tess rushes upstairs, followed by her curious landlady, Mrs. Brooks. When Tess closes her bedroom door, Mrs. Brooks looks through the keyhole. She sees Tess kneeling despairingly, weeping and blaming Alec for tricking her into leaving Angel. "I have lost him now — again because of — you!" she cries. "O God — I can't bear this! — I cannot!"

Mrs. Brooks hears Alec reply sharply, and goes downstairs before she can be discovered. Later, she sees Tess leave the house, dressed as if she were going for a walk. Time passes, and Mrs. Brooks rests in the room beneath the d'Urberville apartment. Suddenly she notices a damp red spot spreading on the ceiling above her. It is blood. Frightened, she calls a workman in from outside and asks him to investigate with her.

When they open the door upstairs, they find Alec lying dead, stabbed through the heart.

Commentary

"Fulfilment," the title of Phase Seven, refers to the way in which the main characters now fulfil the destinies that brought them together. Angel, who rejected Tess, is now rejected by her. As Alec was responsible for Tess' downfall, she will be responsible for his. Too late, Angel tries to make amends. He pays for Durbeyfield's tombstone. He offers money to Mrs. Durbeyfield, but he does not wonder at her comfortable house and good clothes. These improved circumstances are, of course, due to Tess' capitulation to Alec. Once again she has let others make use of her. This time she feels she owes her family Alec's protection because she blames her bad reputation for the eviction from Marlott.

The meeting of the lovers is both stunning and pathetic. Angel, prematurely aged by his illness, looks a wreck of a man. Tess, in her uncaring subjection to Alec, never has looked more beautiful or better cared-for.

Although Alec has provided for Tess as Angel should have, she accuses him of twice cheating her of Angel's love. She has been beaten down and passive, but at the thought that Angel may leave her again, she becomes an avenging Fury. Hardy handles the murder of Alec with subtlety and finesse. We do not see it happen — we are only made aware of it through Mrs. Brooks' reactions. This device makes it believable as lurid melodrama could not.

QUESTION: Was Tess justified in blaming Alec for her loss of Angel?

CHAPTERS 57, 58 AND 59

Summary

After leaving Tess, Angel walks to his hotel, determined to leave Sandbourne. He packs and starts for the station to board a train. Looking back, he sees Tess running after him. She is pale and quivering, but she tells him calmly that she has killed Alec. "I owe it to you and to myself, Angel. . . . He has come between us and ruined us, and now he can never do it any more." She begs Angel to say that he loves her: "you don't know how entirely I was unable to bear your not loving me!"

Angel cannot believe her story of the murder. He thinks she is delirious, but he tells her he loves her very much and will not desert her again. They walk away, out of town, holding each other around the waist. Night comes on, and they hunt for shelter, finally deciding to return to a deserted house they had passed some distance back. Angel crawls through an unlocked window. Upstairs is a furnished bedchamber, and they sink down there to rest.

For five days they hide in the house, avoiding the caretaker when she comes to make her rounds. Tess is happy and childlike. "All is trouble outside there," she says. "Inside here content." When the caretaker discovers them asleep on the sixth morning, she does not have the heart to disturb them. But upon awakening, Angel knows they must move on. He hopes to reach a port from which they can escape.

Night brings them to the vast, ancient ruins of Stonehenge on the Salisbury plain. Tess is too exhausted to go on. She lies down on an oblong slab, sheltered from the wind by a pillar. Angel realizes that she is lying on an altar of the ancient temple. As she rests, she tells him how happy he has made her. She asks him to marry her sister, 'Liza-Lu — "if you lose me, as you will do shortly." 'Liza-Lu, she tells him, "has all the best of me without the bad of me; . . ."

Dawn is breaking when she asks Angel if he thinks they will meet after death. This is contrary to his beliefs, and he does not answer. Saddened, Tess says, "I fear that means no! . . . And I wanted so to see you again. . . ."

She falls asleep, and Angel is left to watch the dawn appear. He sees men moving down across the plain toward them, and knows that they are being surrounded by officers of the law. He realizes that Tess really has killed Alec.

Tess awakens and asks, "Have they come for me?" She does not seem to mind, for she knows her happiness could not last. "I am ready," she says.

Months later, in the city of Wintoncester, a black flag moves slowly up the staff on "an ugly flat-topped octagonal tower." Their faces seemingly "shrunk to half their natural size," 'Liza-Lu and Angel watch the flag from a nearby hillside. As the flag waves upon the breeze, the two watchers bend in prayer. "Justice was done, and the President of the Immortals, in Aeschylean phrase, had ended his sport with Tess." Taking 'Liza-Lu's hand, Angel rises and moves on to pick up the pieces of his shattered life.

Commentary

The gods who sport with Tess at least allow her a few days of happiness under Angel's protection. Once again it is spring (May), the time when Tess has been happy before at Talbothays. The seed for the murder of Alec was unwittingly planted by Angel in Chapter 36, when he told her that if her seducer were dead, they might be able to live together. Undoubtedly, Tess has never forgotten his words, and now she has acted upon them.

Although Angel has learned humility and the ability to feel remorse, there is much of the "old" Angel still about him. He marvels at "the strangeness" of the quality of her love for him, "which has apparently extinguished her moral sense altogether." When she asks him to marry 'Liza-Lu, he objects because she is his sister-in-law. He cannot even agree when Tess asks him about life after death, even though this would give her much comfort.

When Hardy says that Justice was done, he, of course, means "Injustice." He has probably made an allusion to Zeus in his reference to the "President of the Immortals." Zeus was the all-powerful supreme god of the Greeks who enforced morals and punished those who defied him. His name means "sky," and therefore Hardy probably equated him with the unfeeling natural laws of the universe. (Aeschylus was the first of three great Greek poets of tragedy. He is the author of

Agamemnon, among other works. It is interesting that Agamemnon was also murdered by his wife.)

The grim working out of the tragedy leaves its mark on Angel and 'Liza-Lu. Even if they marry, there seems little hope of happiness for them. For Tess, at last, there is rest with the "unknowing d'Urberville knights and dames" whose name brought her so much misery. Notice that Tess' final "sacrifice" is made when she rises from the sacrificial altar at Stonehenge.

QUESTION: Do you think Hardy means to imply that Tess was doomed because of her own weakness or because the hostile universe in which she lived is the enemy of man? Why?

Character Sketches

Tess

Tess is the central character of the book. Her life, for a period of some four years, is presented in detail. Her thoughts about a variety of subjects, and her emotions are explored in all their facets. The other characters are presented only as they affect Tess' life. Her growth and development from a simple, country girl to a complex woman weaves through the novel, while the changes occurring in the men she knows are presented only summarily. The only two characters who never come in contact with Tess are Angel's parents. All the others enter the spotlight only when Tess is also on stage.

In spite of her poverty-stricken background and shiftless parents, Tess exhibits qualities worthy of her illustrious ancestors. She realizes her importance as an individual, and wishes to walk uprightly throughout her life. Her parents seem to recognize her superiority, but they also realize that "she's tractable at bottom."

Tess is often compared to a "bird caught in a trap," and by the repeated use of this metaphor the author pictures his heroine as almost without blame for her sin against society. The "trap" was set both by her parents and by Alec. She is sent out into the world at a very young age, innocent to the dangers which might await her. Her mother, with visions of a fancy marriage for her pretty daughter, gives little thought to the type of man her daughter will be associated with. Her father also thinks only of his own desire to restore the family name to its former stature. Alec takes advantage of her innocence and physical exhaustion to seduce her.

The simplicity and innocence we see in Tess never leave her. Though she remains, as Hardy designated, "a pure woman," Tess herself feels she is unworthy of Angel and "impure" because she has been seduced by Alec; that is why she meekly allows Angel to abandon her.

In spite of her essential *goodness*, Tess is not a featureless goody-goody. She is passionate and sensual, and displays a fierce temper with Alec. She understands the meaning of justice. When Angel refuses to forgive her, she points out to him that she has forgiven him. She destroys Alec's tenuous and new-found faith with Angel's arguments — almost as ruthlessly as Alec once destroyed the order of her life.

Tess' strength is her "aliveness" and her determination to overcome her misfortunes. Her weakness lies in her attitude toward her family and toward Angel. She feels responsible for the welfare of her family, and sacrifices herself for them. Her ability to love and her desire to protect those she loves starts with her family, and ends with Angel. Her love idealizes him and, even when he deserts her, she protects his name with her fierce loyalty.

The tragedy of Tess' life lies in the battle between "the inherent will to enjoy and the circumstantial will against enjoyment." After her brief affair with Alec, she is no longer a simple girl, but her experiences have failed to demoralize her soul. "Unexpended youth rises automatically within her after a temporary check bringing with it hope and an invincible instinct toward self-delight." Her loyalty to the man she loves, and the forbearance and nobility of her struggle against the Fate which rules her life win the respect and sympathies of the reader.

Angel

Angel is an intruder into the Essex country life, and is presented as a human being set apart from those around him. He is no longer comfortable with his clerical family because his semi-emancipated thinking has alienated him from their single-minded approach to life. He joins the agricultural community to prepare for his future life as a farmer, but he is treated as a temporary visitor who will soon be going on to a grander life.

Hardy uses the character of Angel to present many of the controversial subjects of the day. Hardy calls Angel a representative young man of the times, and by that he probably means that Angel is torn by the conflict between science and religion. He considers himself emancipated from the thinking of his clerical father: he is a rationalist, one who wants reasons for everything. But, although Angel rejects Christian philosophy and considers himself an independent thinker, he is an unknowing victim of the conventional morality of his time.

Though Angel takes pride in his understanding and acceptance of the countryfolk, he is deceiving himself about his "independent" thought once again. Even while Tess fits his own concept of a "fresh and virginal daughter of nature," she is not good enough for him. He teaches her manners and speech so that she will not embarrass him when he introduces her to his peers. He maintains contempt for "old names," but the importance to him of Tess' ancestry belies this.

The distinction between religion and morality is a key element of Angel's part in the novel. He personifies the role convention can play in shaping one's destiny. Although intellectually liberated from orthodox Christianity, he is all the more dependent upon the Christian ethic and believes good morals are "the only safeguard for us poor human beings." Idealizing Tess into an essence of virgin purity, Angel is struck dumb when he learns that she, too, has sinned. Her confession strikes at the very foundation of his life. It is not until he removes himself from the society in which he has been raised, and sees morality in its temporal and transitory aspects, that he is able to accept Tess' character as one who wills good, no matter what the deeds.

Although there is a lack of harmony between Angel's feelings and his intellect and values, there is much that is attractive about him. He is gentle, and he impresses Tess with the chivalrous way he treats her and the other milkmaids. Though he abandons Tess, he believes he has made adequate provision for her. Unfortunately, maturity, and with it appreciation of Tess' essential goodness, come to Angel only after he has suffered terrible hardships, and, predictably, they come too late.

Alec

Alec is the evil man in Tess' life, but he has good qualities and he comes through as more of a man than Angel does. His physical description would make him a typical villain in a melodrama. He is tall, with an almost swarthy complexion. A well-groomed, black moustache complete with curled points tops his badly molded, full lips. There are "touches of barbarism in his contours [and] a singular force . . . in his face and in his bold rolling eye."

Alec admits that he is a bad sort of fellow, but can feel genuine remorse at the consequences of his actions. When he drives in such a reckless fashion that Tess refuses to ride with him, he is distressed at the sight of her walking such a distance. He is upset when Tess leaves him, and drives like a madman to help her with her load if she won't come back to him. He is ready to pay for his deeds and urges Tess to write to him if she is in the least difficulty. When they meet again and Tess tells him of the child, he is struck mute.

His desire to master Tess is equalled by his genuine wish to protect and help her. The things that Angel should have done for Tess are done by Alec, even though they may have been done for the wrong reasons. Alec realizes that concern for her brothers and sisters is Tess' weak spot. By helping them he can put her in a position of indebtedness to him. Alec does quite a bit for them in a material way, and is more concerned for their welfare than Angel, whose single contribution is to pay for Jack's headstone.

Not enough of Alec's character is divulged to the reader to make his reappearance as a preacher believable. We have the feeling, rather, that he is merely another instrument in the hands of Fate working to thwart Tess. Supposedly, the influence of Mr. Clare and the death of his mother result in his conversion, "perhaps the mere freak of a careless man in search of a new sensation."

When Tess recites the thoughts of logical Angel, Alec's enthusiasm is stilled. He struggles to hold his shallow faith, but finds that his passion for Tess overwhelms all thoughts of carrying on his preaching. Once his faith is lost, he refuses the hypocrisy of preaching altogether. With a simple change of clothes and a shave, he is reconverted.

His attitude toward Tess is a combination of a desire to master her again and a genuine regard for her welfare. He is troubled by the sight of her agonizing labors on the Flintcomb-Ash farm. He rails against society for its cruel treatment of her family, and he offers to help her in a variety of ways. At the same time, he is angry at her ingratitude and taunts her about her missing husband. He finally wins her back by convincing her that her husband will never return. His fatal mistake is to carry on the taunts once Angel has returned. When he calls Tess' beloved by a foul name, she kills him.

Though Angel is blind to Tess' virtue, Alec is not. "Why I did not despise you was on account of your being unsmirched in spite of all," he tells Tess, and thus acknowledges her moral superiority. It intrigues and challenges him even more than her sexual attractiveness.

Like Angel, Alec is a victim of his own ego. Like Angel, he is self-centered. His passions rule him, but he does feel remorse for the harm he does.

Jack Durbeyfield

Many of Tess' problems can be traced to her parents, whose poverty and shiftlessness make it imperative that she leave her home to find employment at the d'Urbervilles. Jack Durbeyfield is a cut above the farm laborers. He ranks with the artisans of Marlott, "who had formed the backbone of the village life in the past, who were the depositaries of the village traditions." We are told that in days past he had cows and chickens, but his drinking and irregular energy for work led to the decline in family fortunes. He is a haggler when we first meet him, dependent upon an old horse for his livelihood, but he doesn't blame Tess for the death of the horse. He works harder digging a grave for him than he has worked for months growing a crop for the family.

Jack's life is changed by the revelation that he is a descendant of the noble d'Urbervilles. He begins to live as he deems proper for a titled man as soon as he hears of his pedigree. No longer does he consider it proper to slave at common labor. He spends his time thinking of ways to restore his family name to its former grandeur. Since dreaming and foolish scheming are all the effort he cares to make, he lives and dies in poverty.

Jack is not a likable character. It was his drinking which forced Tess to give up her cherished hope of becoming a teacher, and his shiftlessness later makes it necessary for her to leave home. He shows more concern about what his cronies at the Pure Drop Inn will say than about Tess' troubles. When her baby falls ill, his "sensitiveness to the smudge which Tess had set upon [his] nobility" makes him refuse to let her send for the parson. Nowhere in the book does he express concern for anything but his "noble name" and his dubious reputation.

Joan Durbeyfield

Although Joan is as weak and foolish as her husband, she is capable of deeper feelings. She seems to love her husband and to enjoy the rare occasions when she can be alone with him.

Joan is reasonably happy because she refuses to think very much about life in general. She has the happy intelligence of a child and an elastic spirit which bounces back after every setback, whether it be the loss of a crop or the damaged reputation of her daughter. In contrast to Tess, who has received some education at the village school, Joan is steeped in superstition and folklore.

Joan is vain and witless. She prides herself on her pretty face and is proud that Tess has inherited her good looks. She has visions of a fine marriage for her daughter and encourages her daughter to go to work for the good-looking and wealthy d'Urberville. She is affectionate with her children, but feels no great responsibility for them. She appears to have an extra fondness and respect for Tess.

The Reverend Mr. Clare

Hardy says nothing about the physical appearance of Angel's parents. In spite of Hardy's distaste for religion, he draws his portraits of Angel's parents with affection. Perhaps this is because the Clares observe the spirit as well as the form of Christianity. They deny themselves to help their needy parishioners. They would have helped Tess, if she had asked them to.

Mr. Clare is a well-known parson in Wessex. His fame extends beyond his own parish, for he has affected the lives of many people. He is of the Low Church school, Evangelical, and is regarded as extremist even by his contemporaries. He wins the admiration of all for his thoroughness and his great energy in applying his principles.

His fundamentalist theology emphasizes man's sinful nature and the necessity to strive to live a moral, spiritually faithful life. In his unceasing attempts to spread his beliefs, James Clare never thinks of himself, but only of those he can save. His views are rigid and fixed, but his sense of charity and justice is strong. Despite his narrowness, Mr. Clare is described as far less "starched and ironed" than his older sons (who are caricatures of the conventional university graduate).

Mrs. Clare

Essentially a good person, she is inclined to be swayed by the values of a class-conscious society. James Clare never asks about Tess' social position, but Mrs. Clare refers to her as a "mere child of the soil." Her deepest concern, however, is for Tess' moral character.

Felix and Cuthbert Clare

These two young clergymen are narrow-minded, conventional, snobbish, and lacking in humanity. Their designation of Angel's marriage as "unfortunate" is based on their opinion of Tess' social class as "low." Hardy implies that their snobbish stupidity is the result of their university education, which he felt stultified honest emotion and original thought.

Mercy Chant

This cold, prudish young lady, the original choice of the Clares as a wife for Angel, symbolizes everything that Hardy felt was wrong with the practice of religion – the "curiously unnatural sacrifice of humanity to mysticism." The form, the conventions of her religion are all that interest Mercy: she understands nothing of love, faith, kindness, forgiveness, or mercy. Her name is intentionally ironic.

Marian

Good-hearted, slovenly Marian proves her friendship for Tess when she writes to Angel: "Look to your wife if you do love her as much as she do love you." Like her fellow dairymaids, Izz Huett and Retty Priddle, Marian is in love with Angel. When Tess and Angel marry, she takes to drink. "'Tis my only comfort – You see I lost him: you didn't." But when she finds Tess *has* lost Angel, she is kindness itself – finding Tess a job at Flintcomb-Ash and cheering her through the long winter with reminiscences of Talbothays.

Izz Huett

Izz Huett exhibits the same strong feeling of friendship for Tess. When Angel, kicking at convention, asks Izz to run away with him, she tells him how much Tess loves him.

Retty Priddle

Retty does not play as large a part in the story as do Marian and Izz. She is an overemotional girl who tries to drown herself after Angel's marriage. Perhaps her inability to accept the loss of Angel with fatalism is due to her "noble" ancestry. Like Tess, she is descended from noble but extinct lines of aristocracy.

Farmer Groby

Hardy hints at a complex character here. Groby first appears as the man who insults Tess and is beaten by Angel. He therefore bears Tess a grudge and, when he meets her on the road to Flintcomb-Ash, tells her she should beg his pardon for Angel's blows. It is stretching coincidence rather far when he turns up again as Tess' employer at Flintcomb-Ash. There he tells her that he has got the better of her, but Tess is not afraid. His bullying is more welcome than Alec's offers of help. Indeed, Tess says to Alec, "He won't hurt me. *He's* not in love with me."

Mrs. d'Urberville

This amiable lady, elderly and blind, might have reacted with sympathy if Tess had told her about their supposed kinship, but Alec makes sure that she never learns of it. Between mother and son there seems to be an armed truce. Mrs. d'Urberville loves her son, but disapproves of his behavior, though she is powerless to control it. Alec tells Tess he "can't stand" his mother, but is remorseful when she dies.

Literary Elements

Structure

Hardy's novel was originally published in serial form. Thus, each chapter is sparked by an important incident — or sometimes by three or four such incidents. Tess is the most important character, and it is her thoughts, her attempts to overcome adversity, and her final defeat that form the story's plot. There are no subplots. The other characters are portrayed in terms of how their lives touch Tess and how their actions influence her life.

Tess is divided into seven phases. The end of each phase is also the end of an important stage of Tess' life. She begins each phase of her life with an altered view of herself and her destiny. "The Maiden" ends with the loss of Tess' virginity. Phase the Second, "Maiden No More" is concerned with Tess' retreat into her own private world of grief and guilt. It ends as Tess is about to venture out into the world again: she decides to go to Talbothays. The third phase, for obvious reasons, is entitled "The Rally." Angel's confession of his love for Tess brings this period to a close. "The Consequence" is the natural and inevitable result of "The Rally." After much soul-searching, Tess gives in to her love for Angel and marries him. This phase ends with her confession, and is followed, predictably, by "The Woman Pays." Angel leaves Tess and she again withdraws from the world to the purgatory of Flintcomb-Ash. Though it is Angel Tess awaits, this phase ends with her reunion with Alec d'Urberville. The sixth phase is entitled "The Convert." Though this most obviously refers to Alec's conversions to, and then from, religious fanaticism, it also describes Angel's awakened appreciation for Tess' essential virtue. This phase ends when the Durbeyfields find themselves homeless, with no one to turn to but Alec. The seventh phase is ironically called "Fulfilment." Alec has won Tess (after a fashion), but she murders him. Tess gains Angel's protection, as she has always hoped, but she is taken from him to be hanged. Angel has learned to see Tess for what she is, and has won her forgiveness, but he loses her forever.

Setting

The boundaries of Hardy's imaginary Wessex are practically identical with those of the historical Kingdom of the Wessex, which included the present counties of Berkshire, Wiltshire, Somerset, Hampshire, Dorset and Devon in the South of England. Hardy has described this area more extensively than any other English writer. His descriptions of roads, valleys, hamlets, villages, towns, woods, meadows, inns and houses are so realistic that they prompted many fans to research into the actual names of the places mentioned. The names used by Hardy are in many cases changed only slightly from the original.

Wessex, in Hardy's hands, is a dramatically useful device. In this circumscribed world, so familiar to Hardy from boyhood on, the author can focus on the elementary passions of its inhabitants and their closely knit interdependence. The conditions of life Hardy describes are those of his boyhood, when there had been no break in the continuity of memories, habits, and instincts. Many of the difficulties encountered by his characters are a result of the intrusion of machines or of people who do not belong. The migrations of workers to new abodes each Old Lady-Day is a scene of tragedy to Hardy, for it means additional loss of customs, folklore, and dialect.

Tess of the d'Urbervilles is steeped in the history, folklore, and traditions of this area. Hardy often uses vivid description of a particular place to mirror and intensify the inner feelings of his characters. Spring and summer at Talbothays are times of "warm ferments." Nature is so lavish in her gifts that Tess must be excused if she views her new home as a sort of "Paradise Found" and accepts Angel Clare as truly angelic. Flintcomb-Ash is a sterile, starved place, a land of exile. Here, Tess starves herself emotionally through a long, bleak winter. She is lying on one of the ancient stones at Stonehenge, where men once sacrificed to the sun, when the time comes for her own sacrifice.

Style

Hardy's use of language is, at the same time, one of his weaknesses and that which marks his individuality as an author. While his ear for the rustic dialect delighted his contemporaries, it is much less meaningful to the modern reader. Many of his phrases are cumbersome and he uses a number of words which are obsolete. On the other hand, his instinct as a poet causes him to use imaginative words and phrases and to color his scenes vividly with all the overtones and subtleties of the mood in which he regards them. He penetrates beneath the material facts to reveal their imaginative significance and, by infusing mystery and magic into his descriptions, he makes them memorable. He is sensitive to rhythm in his prose and can write eloquently and expressively.

Folk ballads and folk magic were part of Hardy's childhood environment, and their style and content heavily influenced his work. His novels and poems have the stark quality of a ballad. His theme of man crushed by the indifferent forces of Nature and Fate is also reminiscent of a ballad. Tess, the innocent maiden, seduced, abandoned, and waiting for the return of her true love, is like the heroine of an ancient ballad. And, in the best ballad style, her fate partakes of the strange and the mystical: she is haunted by a phantom coach; a fortunetelling book forecasts her future; an unlucky cock crows on the afternoon of her wedding day. These gothic touches were derived from the legends and lore that Hardy grew up with.

Hardy's intense interest in the classics is reflected in the many allusions to mythology scattered throughout *Tess*. In Chapter 2, the Marlott May Day festivities are compared to the ancient observances in honor of Ceres, the Roman goddess of agriculture. (The May Day celebration does, of course, have its origins in this pre-Christian festival, and thus Hardy conveys a sense of the truly ancient traditions and roots of his Wessex people.) During the wild revel at the hay trussers in Chapter 10, the workers are transformed into nymphs and pursuing satyrs ("a multiplicity of Pans whirling a multiplicity of Syrinxes"). In Chapter 20, Angel compares Tess to Artemis, Greek goddess of the hunt, and to Demeter, goddess of the harvest.

Almost as numerous as his classical allusions are the Biblical references Hardy includes in *Tess*. In Chapter 19, Tess compares herself to the "poor Queen of Sheba who lived in the Bible" when she speaks of all that Angel has read and seen. She is equating Angel with the wise Solomon and herself with the barbaric Sheba. In Chapter 20, Angel thinks of himself as Adam and of Tess as Eve. Hardy injects the ironic suggestion that Tess is more like "the Magdalen." In Chapter 23, when Angel carries the other three dairymaids and Tess across the pool of water, he whispers to Tess, "Three Leahs to get one Rachel." In the Bible, Jacob labors for seven years to win the hand of Rachel, but is tricked, and marries her sister, Leah, instead. He has to work for seven more years to win Rachel. In Chapter 51, Hardy refers to the bondage the Israelites suffered in Egypt to explain the increased movement of families from farm to farm and job to job. "The Egypt of one family was the Land of Promise to the family who saw it from a distance, till by residence there it became in turn their Egypt also; and so they changed and changed."

It is a tribute to Hardy's art that these allusions enrich rather then encumber. As might be expected of one of England's major poets, Hardy is able to use the emotional intensity of poetic language to sustain and emphasize the structure of his novel.

Symbolism

Hardy is an expert at developing symbolic patterns so that the reader readily makes associations between objects of everyday life and invisible qualities or attitudes. The birds which have literally been run to earth in Chapter 41 symbolize Tess' feeling of being hunted, and foreshadow the time when she will be "run to earth" at Stonehenge. When she lies on the slab at Stonehenge, she becomes one with history's millions of victims; its immensity and age dwarf her. Hardy's symbolism again expresses his vision of human destiny overwhelmed by the indifferent universal forces.

Folklore and folk magic play a large part in the interpretation of symbolism. Omens — signs which foretell the future — abound in *Tess*.

The thorn in the roses Alec gives Tess pricks her chin. This is an omen of the blood to be shed between them. The evil portraits of the d'Urberville women that unaccountably reflect Tess' own features are the ominous symbols of the evil the d'Urberville name has reflected upon her. Angel's name suggests his spiritual nature — but it also suggests something which is not "human." When he plays his harp in the evil-smelling, blighted garden at Talbothays, we are forewarned that something is wrong, that he cannot be the near-perfect man he appears to be.

The different settings in *Tess* have value as symbols. The turnip field at Flintcomb-Ash resembles the featureless face of "a desolate drab." The sky above it "wore, in another color, the same likeness; a white vacuity of countenance with the lineaments gone. So these two upper and nether visages confronted each other all day long, the white face looking down on the brown face, and the brown face looking up at the white face, without anything standing between them but the two girls crawling over the surface of the former like flies."

Grotesque Imagery

Hardy makes use of a grotesque imagery to provide the reader with a more penetrating vision. A good example of this may be seen in Chapter 19, where Tess walks in the garden listening to the sound of Angel's music. She is fascinated and draws closer to the performer. Supposedly, this is the beginning of love, but as she walks she gathers cuckoo-spittle on her skirts, cracks snails that are underfoot, stains her hands with thistle-milk and slug-slime, and rubs off her naked arms sticky blights. Can this overgrown garden perhaps suggest an impending catastrophe? Surely the images are ironically incongruous with the happiness Hardy is talking about.

Another example may be found in Chapter 27, when Angel sees the inside of Tess' mouth "as if it had been a snake's." In the midst of the Talbothays idyll — the Garden of Eden — there is a hint of evil and betrayal.

This imagery is unexpected, evocative, and effective in bringing to the reader a more significant esthetic experience.

Point of View

Hardy is the omniscient narrator of the tale of Tess. He knows everything about her: her secret thoughts, her motives, her feelings about and reaction to people and events. He is definitely her advocate and, at many points, he intrudes into the story to explain or justify or comment on her actions. He tells us almost all he knows about Tess. He does not know all about some of the lesser characters and tells us only what is significant to the story of Tess about any of them.

Much of the story is told in summary narrative form. Only during the idyll of the Talbothays dairy, while the love between Angel and Tess is developing, is there an extended pictorial presentation.

*Colour and Movement in Hardy's
Tess of the d'Urbervilles

> ". . . the discontinuance of immobility in any
> quarter suggested confusion."
>
> (*Return of the Native*)
>
> ". . . the least irregularity of motion startled
> her. . . ." (*Tess of the d'Urbervilles*)

I

Every great writer has his own kind of legibility, his own way of turning life into a language of particular saliences, and in Hardy this legibility is of a singularly stark order. If we can think of a novelist as creating, among other things, a particular linguistic world by a series of selective intensifications of our shared vocabulary, then we can say that Hardy's world is unusually easy to read. The key words in his dialect, to continue the image, stand out like braille. It is as though some impersonal process of erosion had worn away much of the dense circumstantial texture of his tales, revealing the basic resistant contours of a sequence of events which Hardy only has to point to to make us see — like ancient marks on a barren landscape. And Hardy above all does make us see. Just as he himself could not bear to be touched, so he does not "touch" the people and things in his tales, does not interfere with them or absorb them into his own sensibility. When he says in his introduction to *Tess of the d'Urbervilles* that "a novel is an impression, not an argument," or in his introduction to *Jude the Obscure* that "like former productions of this pen, *Jude the Obscure* is simply an endeavour to give shape and coherence to a series of seemings, or personal impressions," we should give full stress to the idea of something seen but not tampered with, something scrupulously watched in its otherness, something perceived but not made over. Hardy's famous, or notorious, philosophic broodings and asides are part of his reactions as a watcher, but they never give the impression of violating the people and objects of which his tale is composed. Reflection and perception are kept separate (in Lawrence they often tend to merge), and those who complain about the turgidity of his thoughts may be overlooking the incomparable clarity of his eyes.

II

This illusion that the tale exists independently of Hardy's rendering of it *is* of course only an illusion, but it testifies to art of a rather special

*From *Critical Quarterly*, X, 1968 (pp. 219-239). Copyright © by Tony Tanner. Reprinted by permission of the author and publisher.

kind. For all Henry James's scrupulous indirectness, Hardy's art is more truly impersonal. He goes in for graphic crudities of effect which James would have scorned, yet, as other critics have testified, the result is an anonymity which we more commonly associate with folk-tale, or the ballads. By graphic crudity of effect I am referring, for instance, to such moments as when Tess, shortly after being seduced, encounters a man who is writing in large letters "THY, DAMNATION, SLUMBERETH, NOT." There are commas between every word "as if to give pause while that word was driven well home to the reader's heart." This is not unlike Hardy's own art which is full of prominent notations, and emphatic pauses which temporarily isolate, and thus vivify, key incidents and objects. On the level of everyday plausibility and probability it is too freakish a chance which brings Tess and the painted words together at this point. In the vast empty landscapes of Hardy's world, peoples' paths cross according to some more mysterious logic — that same imponderable structuring of things in time which brought the *Titanic* and the ice-berg together at one point in the trackless night sea. (See the poem "The Convergence of the Twain.") A comparable "crudity" is discernible in the characterisation which is extremely schematic, lacking in all the minute mysteries of individual uniqueness which a writer like James pursued. *Angel* Clare is indeed utterly ethereal; his love is "more spiritual than animal." He even plays the harp! On the other hand Alec d'Urberville is almost a stage villain with his "swarthy complexion ... full lips ... well-groomed black moustache with curled points," his cigars and his rakish way with his fast spring-cart. If we turn from character to plot sequence we see at once that the overall architecture of the novel is blocked out with massive simplicity in a series of balancing phases — The Maiden, Maiden No More; The Rally, The Consequence; and so on. Let it be conceded at once that Hardy's art is not subtle in the way that James and many subsequent writers are subtle. Nevertheless I think it is clear that Hardy derives his great power from that very "crudity" which, in its impersonal indifference to plausibility and rational cause and effect, enhances the visibility of the most basic lineaments of the tale.

III

I want first to concentrate on one series of examples which shows how this manifest visibility works. For an artist as visually sensitive as Hardy, colour is of the first importance and significance, and there is one colour which literally catches the eye, and is meant to catch it, throughout the book. This colour is red, the colour of blood, which is associated with Tess from first to last. It dogs her, disturbs her, destroys her. She is full of it, she spills it, she loses it. Watching Tess's life we begin to see that her destiny is nothing more or less than the colour red. The first time we (and Angel) see Tess, in the May dance with the other girls, she stands out. How? They are all in white except that Tess "wore a red ribbon in her hair, and was the only one of the white company who would boast of such a pronounced adornment." Tess is marked, even from the happy valley of her birth and childhood. The others are a semi-anonymous mass; Tess already has that heightened legibility, that eye-taking prominence which suggests that she has in some mysterious way been singled out. And the red stands out because it is on a pure white background. In that simple scene and colour contrast is the embryo of the whole book and all that happens in it.

This patterning of red and white is often visible in the background of the book. For instance "The ripe hue of the red and dun kine absorbed the evening sunlight, which the white-coated animals returned to the eye in rays almost dazzling, even at the distant elevation on which she stood." This dark red and dazzling white is something seen, it is something there; it is an effect on the retina, it is a configuration of matter. In looking at this landscape Tess in fact is seeing the elemental mixture which conditions her own existence. In the second chapter Tess is described as "a mere vessel of emotion untinctured by experience." The use of the word "untinctured" may at first seem surprising; we perhaps tend to think of people being shaped by experience rather than coloured by it — yet the use of a word connected with dye and paint is clearly intentional. In her youth Tess is often referred to as a "white shape" — almost more as a colour value in a landscape than a human being. And on the night of her rape she is seen as a "white muslin figure" sleeping on a pile of dead leaves; her "beautiful feminine tissue" is described as "practically blank as snow." The historic precedent for what is to happen to this vulnerable white shape is given at the start when we read that "the Vale was known in former times as the Forest of White Hart, from a curious legend of King Henry III's reign, in which the killing by a certain Thomas de le Lynd of a beautiful white hart which the king had run down and spared, was made the occasion of a heavy fine." Against all social injunctions, white harts are brought down. And in Tess's case the "tincturing" — already prefigured in the red ribbon — starts very early.

The next omen — for even that harmless ribbon is an omen in this world — occurs when Tess drives the hives to market when her father is too drunk to do the job. When she sets out the road is still in darkness. Tess drifts, sleeps, dreams. Then there is the sudden collision and she wakes to find that Prince, their horse, has been killed by another cart. "The pointed shaft of the cart had entered the breast of the unhappy Prince like a sword, and from the wound his life's blood was spouting in a stream and falling with a hiss on the road. In her despair Tess sprang forward and put her hand upon the hole, with the only result that she became splashed from face to skirt with the crimson drops. Then she stood helplessly looking on. Prince also stood firm and motionless as long as he could; till he suddenly sank down in a heap." It is possible to say different things about this passage. On one level the death of the horse means that the family is destitute, which means in turn that Tess will have to go begging to the d'Urbervilles. Thus, it is part of a rough cause and effect economic sequence. But far more graphic, more disturbing and memorable, is the image of the sleeping girl on the darkened road, brutally awakened and desperately trying to staunch a fatal puncture, trying to stop the blood which cannot be stopped and only getting drenched in its powerful spurts. It adumbrates the loss of her virginity, for she, too, will be brutally pierced on a darkened road far from home, and once the blood of her innocence has been released, she too, like the stoical Prince, will stay upright as long as she can until, all blood being out, she will sink down suddenly in a heap. Compressed in that one imponderable scene we can see her whole life.

After this Tess is constantly encountering the colour red — if not literal blood, manifold reminders of it. When she approaches the d'Urberville house we read: "It was of recent erection — indeed almost new — and of the same rich red colour that formed such a contrast with the evergreens of the lodge." And the corner of the house "rose like a geranium bloom against the subdued colours around." Tess, with her red ribbon, also stood out against "the subdued colours around." Mysteriously, inevitably, this house will play a part in her destiny. And if this red house contains her future rapist, so it is another red house which contains her final executioner, for the prison where she is hanged is "a large red-brick building." Red marks the houses of sex and death. When first she has to approach the leering, smoking Alec d'Urberville, he forces roses and strawberries on her, pushing a strawberry into her mouth, pressing the roses into her bosom. Hardy, deliberately adding to the legibility I am describing, comments that d'Urberville is one "who stood fair to be the blood-red ray in the spectrum of her young life." On the evening of the rape, Tess is first aware of d'Urberville's presence at the dance when she sees "the red coal of a cigar." This is too clearly phallic to need comment, but it is worth pointing out that, from the first, d'Urberville seems to have the power of reducing Tess to a sort of trance-like state, he envelopes her in a "blue narcotic haze" of which his cigar smoke is the most visible emblem. On the night of the rape, at the dance, everything is in a "mist," like "illuminated smoke"; there is a "floating, fusty *debris* of peat and hay" stirred up as "the panting shapes spun onwards." Everything together seems to form "a sort of vegeto-human pollen." In other words it becomes part of a basic natural process in which Tess is caught up simply by being alive, fecund, and female. D'Urberville is that figure, that force, at the heart of the haze, the mist, the smoke, waiting to claim her when the dance catches her up (we first saw her at a dance and she can scarcely avoid being drawn in). It is in a brilliant continuation of this blurred narcotic atmosphere that Hardy has the rape take place in a dense fog, while Tess is in a deep sleep. Consciousness and perception are alike engulfed and obliterated. When Tess first leaves d'Urberville's house she suddenly wakes up to find that she is covered in roses; while removing them a thorn from a remaining rose pricks her chin. "Like all the cottagers in Blackmoor Vale, Tess was steeped in fancies and prefigurative superstitions; she thought this an ill omen." The world of the book is indeed a world of omens (*not* symbols) in which things and events echo and connect in patterns deeper than lines of rational cause and effect. Tess takes it as an omen when she starts to bleed from the last rose pressed on her by Alec. She is right; for later on she will again wake up to find that he has drawn blood — in a way which determines her subsequent existence.

After the rape we are still constantly seeing the colour red. The man who writes up the words promising damnation is carrying "a tin pot of red paint in his hand." As a result "these vermilion words shone forth." Shortly after, when Tess is back at home, Hardy describes a sunrise in which the sun "broke through chinks of cottage shutters, throwing stripes like red-hot pokers upon cupboards, chests of drawers, and other furniture within." (The conjunction of sunlight and redness is a phenomenon I will return to.) And Hardy goes on: "But of all ruddy things that morning the brightest were two broad arms of painted wood ... forming the revolving Maltese cross of the reaping-machine." We will later see Tess virtually trapped and tortured on a piece of red machinery, and her way will take her past several crosses until she finds her own particular sacrificial place. When Tess is working in the fields her flesh again reveals its vulnerability. "A bit of her naked arm is visible between the buff leather of the gauntlet and the sleeve of her gown; and as the day wears on its feminine smoothness becomes scarified by the stubble, and bleeds." Notice the shift to the present tense: Hardy makes us look at the actual surfaces — the leather, the sleeve, the flesh, the blood. One of the great strengths of Hardy is that he knew, and makes us realise, just how very much the surfaces of things mean.

Of course it is part of the whole meaning of the book that there is as much red inside Tess as outside her. Both the men who seek to possess her see it. When Tess defies d'Urberville early on, she speaks up at him, "revealing the red and ivory of her mouth"; while when Angel watches her unawares, "she was yawning, and he saw the red interior of her mouth as if it had been a snake's." When Angel does just kiss her arm, and he kisses the inside vein, we read that she was such a "sheaf of susceptibilities" that "her blood [was] driven to her finger ends." Tess does not so much act as re-act. She would be content to be passive, but something is always disturbing her blood, and all but helplessly she submits to the momentums of nature in which, by her very constitution, she is necessarily involved. As for example when she is drawn by Angel's music "like a fascinated bird" and she makes her way through, once again, a misty atmosphere ("mists of pollen") of uncontrollable swarming fertility and widespread insemination. It is a place of growth, though not wholly a place of beauty. There are "tall blooming weeds" giving off "offensive smells" and some of the weeds are a bright "red." "She went stealthily as a cat through this profusion of growth, gathering cuckoo-spittle on her skirts, cracking snails that were underfoot, staining her hands with thistle-milk and slug-slime, and rubbing off upon her naked arms sticky blights which though snow-white on the appletree trunks, made *madder* stains on her skin. . . ." (my italics). In some of the earlier editions (certainly up to the 1895 edition) that final phrase was "blood-red stains on her skin"; only later did Hardy change "blood-red" to "madder," a crimson dye made from a climbing plant. This change clearly reveals that he intended us once again to see Tess's arm marked with red, though he opted for a word which better suggested something in nature staining, "tincturing," Tess as she pushes on through "this profusion of growth." And once again Hardy presents us with redness and snow-whiteness in the same scene — indeed, in the same plant.

After Tess has been abandoned by Angel and she has to renew her endless journeying the red omens grow more vivid, more violent. She seeks shelter one night under some bushes and when she wakes up: "Under the trees several pheasants lay about, their rich plummage dabbled with blood; some were dead, some feebly twitching a wing, some staring up at the sky, some pulsating quickly, some contorted, some stretched out — all of them writhing in agony, except for the fortunate ones whose torture had ended during the night by the inability of nature to bear more." There is much that is horribly apposite for Tess in these bloody writhings. (It is worth noting that Hardy uses the same word to describe the torments of the onset of sexual impulse; thus he describes the sleeping girls at Talbothays who are suffering from "hopeless passion." "They writhed feverishly under the oppressiveness of an emotion thrust on them by cruel Nature's law — an emotion which they had neither expected nor desired." The writhings of life are strangely similar to the writhings of death). Looking at the dying birds Tess reprimands herself for feeling self-pity, saying "I be not mangled, and I be not bleeding." But she will be both, and she, too, will have to endure until she reaches "the inability of nature to bear more." Like the white hart and the pheasants she is a hunted animal; hunted not really by a distinct human individual, but by ominous loitering presences like the cruel gun-men she used to glimpse stalking through the woods and bushes — a male blood-letting force which is abroad. Later when she makes her fruitless trek to Angel's parents she sees "a piece of blood-stained paper, caught up from some meat-buyer's dust heap, beat up and down the road without the gate; too flimsy to rest, too heavy to fly away, and a few straws to keep it company." It is another deliberate omen. Tess, too, is blood-stained, she, too, is beat up and down the road outside the gate (she has no home or refuge, no door opens to her); and she, too, very exactly, is too flimsy to rest, too heavy to fly away. (Cf. Eustacia Vye's envy of the heron. "Up in the zenith where he was seemed a free and happy place, away from all contact with the earthly ball to which she was pinioned; and she wished that she could arise uncrushed from its surface and fly as he flew then.") The blood-stained piece of paper is not a clumsy symbol; it is one of a number of cumulative omens. When Alec d'Urberville renews his pressure on Tess, at one point she turns and slashes him across the face with her heavy leather gauntlet. "A scarlet oozing appeared where her blow had alighted and in a moment the blood began dropping from his mouth upon the straw." (Notice again the conjunction of blood and straw.) The man who first made her bleed now stands bleeding from the lips. Blood has blood, and it will have more blood. We need only to see the scene — there, unanalysed, unexplained; a matter of violent movement, sudden compulsions. Hardy spends more time describing the glove than attempting to unravel the hidden thoughts of these starkly confronted human beings. Few other writers can so make us feel that the world is its own meaning — and mystery, requiring no interpretative gloss. Seeing the heavy glove, the sudden blow, the dripping blood, we see all we need to see.

At one point shortly before her marriage, Tess comes into proximity with a railway engine. "No object could have looked more foreign to the gleaming cranks and wheels than this unsophisticated girl, with the round bare arms. . . ." This feeling that her vulnerable flesh is somehow menaced by machinery is realised when she is later set to work on that "insatiable swallower," the relentless threshing machine. It is a bright machine, and the "immense stack of straw" which it is turning out is seen as "the *faeces* of the same buzzing red glutton." Tess is "the only woman whose place was upon the machine so as to be shaken bodily by its spinning." She is beaten into a "stupefied reverie in which her arms worked on independently of her consciousness" (this separation, indeed severance, of consciousness and body is a crucial part of Tess's experience). Whenever she looks up "she beheld always the great upgrown straw-stack, with the men in short-sleeves upon it, against the grey north sky; in front of it the long red elevator like a Jacob's ladder, on which a perpetual stream of threshed straw ascended. . . ." There it is. We see Tess, trapped and stupefied in the cruel red man-made machine. Whenever she looks up in her trance of pain and weariness she sees — the long red elevator, the growing heap of straw, the men at work against the grey sky. It is a scene which is, somehow, her life: the men, the movement, the redness, the straw (blood and straw seem almost to be the basic materials of existence in the book — the vital pulsating fluid, and the dry, dead stalks). At the end of the day she is as a "bled calf." We do not need any enveloping and aiding words; only the legibility of vibrant, perceived detail.

The end of the book is sufficiently well known, but it is worth pointing out how Hardy continues to bring the colour red in front of our eyes. The landlady who peeps through the keyhole during Tess's anguish when Angel has returned reports that, "her lips were bleeding from the clench of her teeth upon them." It is the landlady who sees "the oblong white ceiling, with this scarlet blot in the midst," which is at once the evidence of the murder and the completion of a life which also started with a red patch on a white background, only then it was simply a ribbon on a dress. The blood stain on the ceiling has "the appearance of a gigantic ace of hearts." In that shape of the heart, sex and death are merged in utmost legibility. After this we hardly need to see the hanging. It is enough that we see Tess climb into a vast bed with "crimson damask hangings," not indeed in a home, for she has no home, but in an empty house to be "Let Furnished." And in that great crimson closed-in bed she finds what she has wanted for so long — rest and peace. Apart from the last scene at Stonehenge, we can say that at this point the crimson curtains do indeed fall on Tess; for if she was all white at birth, she is to be all red at death. The massed and linking red omens have finally closed in on Tess and her wanderings are over.

Tess is a "pure woman" as the subtitle, which caused such outrage, specifically says. The purest woman contains tides of blood (Tess is always blushing), and if the rising of blood is sexual passion and the spilling of blood is death, then we can see that the purest woman is sexual and mortal. Remember Tess watching Prince bleed to death — "the hole in his chest looking scarcely large enough to have let out all that animated him." It is not a large hole that Alec makes in Tess when he rapes her, but from then on the blood is bound to go on flowing until that initial violation will finally "let out all that animated her." Hardy is dealing here with the simplest and deepest of matters. Life starts in sex and ends in death, and Hardy constantly shows how closely allied the two forms of blood-letting are in one basic, unalterable rhythm of existence.

IV

I have suggested that the destiny of Tess comes to us as a cumulation of visible omens. It is also a convergence of omens and to explain what I mean I want to add a few comments on the part played in her life by the sun, altars and tombs, and finally walking and travelling. When we first see Tess with the other dancing girls we read that they are all bathed in sunshine. Hardy, ever conscious of effects of light, describes how their hair reflects various colours in the sunlight. More, "as each and all of them were warmed without by the sun, so each of them had a private little sun for her soul to bask in." They are creatures of the sun, warmed and nourished by the source of all heat and life. Tess starts sun-blessed. At the dairy, the sun is at its most active as a cause of the fertile surgings which animate all nature. "Rays from the sunrise drew forth the buds and stretched them into stalks, lifted up sap in noiseless streams, opened petals, and sucked out scents in invisible jets and breathings." This is the profoundly sensuous atmosphere in which Tess, despite mental hesitations, blooms into full female ripeness. Hardy does something very suggestive here in his treatment of the times of day. Tess and Angel rise very early, before the sun. They seem to themselves "the first persons up of all the world." The light is still "half-compounded, aqueous," as though the business of creating animated forms has not yet begun. They are compared to Adam and Eve. As so often when Tess is getting involved with the superior power of a man, the atmosphere is misty, but this time it is cold mist, the sunless fogs which precede the dawn. In this particular light of a cool watery whiteness, Tess appears to Angel as "a visionary essence of woman," something ghostly, "merely a soul at large." He calls her, among other things, Artemis (who lived, of course, in perpetual celibacy). In this sunless light Tess appears to Angel as unsexed, sexless, the sort of non-physical spiritualised essence he, in his impotent spirituality, wants. (At the end he marries a spiritualized image of "Tess.") But Tess is inescapably flesh and blood. And when the sun does come up, she reverts from divine essence to physical milkmaid: "her teeth, lips and eyes scintillated in the sunbeams, and she was again the dazzlingly fair dairymaid only. . . ." (That placing of "only" is typical of the strength of Hardy's prose.) Soon after this, the dairyman tells his story of the seduction of a young girl; "none of them but herself seemed to see the sorrow of it." And immediately we read, "the evening sun was now ugly to her, like a great inflamed wound in the sky." Sex is a natural instinct which however can lead to lives of utter misery. The same sun that blesses, can curse.

Tess drifts into marriage with Angel (her most characteristic way of moving in a landscape is a "quiescent glide"), because "every wave of her blood . . . was a voice that joined with nature in revolt against her scrupulousness," but meanwhile "at half-past six the sun settled down upon the levels, with the aspect of a great forge in the heavens." This suggests not a drawing-up into growth, but a slow inexorable downward crushing force, through an image linked to that machinery which will later pummel her body. It is as though the universe turns metallic against Tess, just as we read when Angel rejects her that there is in him a hard negating force "like a vein of metal in a soft loam." This is the metal which her soft flesh runs up against. Other omens follow on her journey towards her wedding. Her feeling that she has seen the d'Urberville coach before; the postillion who takes them to church and who has "a permanent running wound on the outside of his right leg"; the ominous "afternoon crow" and so on. I want to point to another omen, when the sun seems to single out Tess in a sinister way. It is worth reminding ourselves that when Angel finally does propose to Tess she is quite sun-drenched. They are standing on the "red-brick" floor and the sun slants in "upon her inclining face, upon the blue veins of her temple, upon her naked arm, and her neck, and into the depths of her hair." Now, on what should be the first night of her honeymoon we read: "The sun was so low on that short, last afternoon of the year that it shone in through a small opening and formed a golden staff which stretched across to her skirt, where it made a spot like a paint-mark set upon her." She has been marked before — first, with the blood of a dying beast, now with a mark from the setting sun. We find other descriptions of how the sun shines on Tess subsequently, but let us return to that crimson bed which, I suggested, effectively marked the end of Tess's journey. "A shaft of dazzling sunlight glanced into the room, revealing heavy, old-fashioned furniture, crimson damask hangings, and an enormous four-poster bedstead. . . ." The sun and the redness which have marked Tess's life, now converge at the moment of her approaching death. Finally Tess takes her last rest on the altar of Stonehenge. She speaks to Angel — again, it is before dawn, that sunless part of the day when he can communicate with her.

" 'Did they sacrifice to God here?' asked she.
'No', said he.
'Who to?'
'I believe to the sun. That lofty stone set away by itself is in
the direction of the sun, which will presently rise behind it.' "

When the sun does rise it also reveals the policemen closing in, for it is society which demands a specific revenge upon Tess. But in the configuration of omens which, I think, is the major part of the book, Tess is indeed a victim, sacrificed to the sun. The heathen temple is fitting, since of course Tess is descended from Pagan d'Urberville, and Hardy makes no scruple about asserting that women "retain in their souls far more of the Pagan fantasy of their remote forefathers than of the systematized religion taught their race at a later date." This raises an important point. Is Tess a victim of society, or of nature? Who wants her blood, who is after her, the policemen, or the sun? Or are they in some sadistic conspiracy so that we see nature and society converging on Tess to destroy her? I will return to this question.

To the convergence of redness and the sun we must add the great final fact of the altar, an altar which Tess approaches almost gratefully, and on which she takes up her sacrificial position with exhausted relief. She says (I have run some of her words to Angel together): " 'I don't want to go any further, Angel. . . . Can't we bide here? . . . you used to say at Talbothays that I was a heathen. So now I am at home . . . I like very much to be here.' " Fully to be human is partly to be heathen, as the figure of Tess on the altar makes clear. (And after all what did heathen originally mean? — someone who lived on the heath; and what was a pagan? — someone who lived in a remote village. The terms only acquire their opprobrium after the advent of Christianity. Similarly Hardy points out that Sunday was originally the sun's day — a spiritual superstructure has been imposed on a physical source.) Tess's willingness to take her place on the stone of death has been manifested before. After she returns from the rape we read "her depression was then terrible, and she could have hidden herself in a tomb." On her marriage night, Angel sleepwalks into her room, saying " 'Dead! Dead! Dead! . . . My wife — dead, dead!' " He picks her up, kisses her (which he can now only manage when he is unconscious), and carries her over a racing river. Tess almost wants to jog him so that they can fall to their deaths: but Angel can negotiate the dangers of turbulent water just as he can suppress all passion. His steps are not directed towards the movement of the waters but to the stillness of stone. He takes Tess and lays her in an "empty stone coffin" in the "ruined choir." In Angel's life of suppressed spontaneity and the negation of passional feeling, this is the most significant thing that he does. He encoffins the sexual instinct, then lies down beside Tess. The deepest inclinations of his psyche, his very being, have been revealed.

Later on, when things are utterly desperate for Tess's family and they literally have no roof over their heads, they take refuge by the church in which the family vaults are kept (where "the bones of her ancestors — her useless ancestors — lay entombed"). In their exhaustion they erect an old "four-post bedstead" over the vaults. We see again the intimate proximity of the bed and the grave. This sombre contiguity also adumbrates the ambiguous relief which Tess later finds in her crimson four-post-bed which is also very close to death. On this occasion Tess enters the church and pauses by the "tombs of the family" and "the door of her ancestral sepulchre." It is at this point that one of the tomb effigies moves, and Alec plays his insane jest on her by appearing to leap from a tomb. Again, we are invited to make the starkest sort of comparison without any exegesis from Hardy. Angel, asleep, took Tess in his arms and laid her in a coffin. Alec, however, seems to wake up from the tomb, a crude but animated threat to Tess in her quest for peace. Angel's instinct towards stillness is countered by Alec's instinct for sexual motion. Together they add up to a continuous process in which Tess is simply caught up. For it is both men who drive Tess to her death: Angel by his spiritualised rejection, Alec by his sexual attacks. It is notable that both these men are also cut off from any fixed community; they have both broken away from traditional attitudes and dwellings. Angel roams in his thought; Alec roams in his lust. They are both drifters of the sort who have an unsettling, often destructive impact in the Hardy world.

Tess is a pure product of nature; but she is nature subject to complex and contradictory pressures. Angel wants her spiritual image without her body (when he finds out about her sexual past he simply denies her identity " 'the woman I have been loving is not you' "); Alec wants only her body and is indifferent to anything we might call her soul, her distinctly human inwardness. The effect of this opposed wrenching on her wholeness is to induce a sort of inner rift which develops into something we would now call schizophrenia. While still at Talbothays she says one day: " 'I do know that our souls can be made to go outside our bodies when we are alive.' " Her method is to fix the mind on a remote star and " 'you will soon find that you are hundreds and hundreds o' miles away from your body, which you don't seem to want at all.' " The deep mystery by which consciousness can seek to be delivered from the body which sustains it, is one which Hardy had clearly before him. That an organism can be generated which then wishes to repudiate the very grounds of its existence obviously struck Hardy as providing a very awesome comment on the nature of nature. Tess is robbed of her integrated singleness, divided by two men, two forces. (This gives extra point to the various crosses she passes on her travels; the cross not only indicating torture, but that opposition between the vertical and the horizontal which, as I shall try to show, is ultimately the source of Tess's — and man's — sufferings in Hardy.) It is no wonder that when Alec worries and pursues her at the very door of her ancestors' vault, she should bend down and whisper that line of terrible simplicity — " 'Why am I on the wrong side of this door?' " (A relevant poem of great power is "A Wasted Illness" of which I quote three stanzas which are very apt for Tess:

"Where lies the end
To this foul way?" I asked with weakening breath.
Thereon ahead I saw a door extend —
    The door to Death.

It loomed more clear:
"At last!" I cried. "The all-delivering door!"
And then, I know not how, it grew less near
    Than theretofore.

And back slid I
Along the galleries by which I came,
And tediously the day returned, and sky,
    And life — the same.)

Tess at this moment is utterly unplaced, with no refuge and no comfort. She can only stumble along more and rougher roads; increasingly vulnerable, weary and helpless, increasingly remote from her body. Her only solution is to break through that "all-delivering door," the door from life to death which opens on the only home left to her. This she does, by stabbing Alec and then taking her place on the ritual altar. She has finally spilled all the blood that tormented her; she can then abandon the torments of animateness and seek out the lasting repose she has earned.

V

This brings me to what is perhaps the most searching of all Hardy's preoccupations — walking, travelling, movement of all kinds. Somewhere at the heart of his vision is a profound sense of what we may call the mystery of motion. *Tess of the d'Urbervilles* opens with a man staggering on rickety legs down a road, and it is his daughter we shall see walking throughout the book. Phase the Second opens, once again, simply with an unexplained scene of laboured walking. "The basket was heavy and the bundle was large, but she lugged them along like a person who did not find her especial burden in material things. Occasionally she stopped to rest in a mechanical way by some gate or post; and then, giving the baggage another hitch upon her full round arm, went steadily on again." Such visualised passages carry the meaning of the novel, even down to the material burdens which weigh down that plump, vulnerable flesh: the meaning is both mute and unmistakable. At the start of Phase the Third, again Tess moves: "she left her home for the second time." At first the journey seems easy and comfortable in "a hired trap"; but soon she gets out and walks, and her journey again leads her into portents of the life ahead of her. "The journey over the intervening uplands and lowlands of Egdon, when she reached them, was a more troublesome walk than she had anticipated, the distance being actually but a few miles. It was two hours, owing to sundry turnings, 'ere she found herself on a summit commanding the long-sought-for vale. . . ." The road to the peaceful vale of death is longer and harder than she thinks. Always Tess has to move, usually to harsher and more punishing territories, and always Hardy makes sure we *see* her. After Angel has banished her: "instead of a bride with boxes and trunks which others bore, we see her a lonely woman with a basket and a bundle in her own porterage. . . ." Later she walks to Emminster Vicarage on her abortive journey to see Angel's parents. She starts off briskly but by the end she is weary, and there are omens by the way. For instance, from one eminence she looks down at endless little fields, "so numerous that they look from this height like the meshes of a net." And again she passes a stone cross, Cross-in-Hand, which stands "desolate and silent, to mark the site of a miracle, or murder, or both." (Note the hint of the profound ambivalence and ambiguity of deeds and events.) At the end of this journey there is nobody at home and there follows the incident of Tess losing her walking boots, another physical reminder that the walking gets harder and harder for her. "Her journey back was rather a meander than a march. It had no sprightliness, no purpose; only a tendency." Her movements do get more leaden throughout, and by the end Hardy confronts us with one of the strangest phenomena of existence — motion without volition. (Interestingly enough, Conrad approaches the same phenomenon in *The Secret Agent* where walking is also the most insistent motif.) The only relief in her walking is that as it gets harder it also approaches nearer to darkness. Thus when she is summoned back to her family: "She plunged into the chilly equinoctial darkness ... for her fifteen miles' walk under the steely stars"; and later during this walk from another eminence she "looked from that height into the abyss of chaotic shade which was all that revealed itself of the vale on whose further side she was born." She is indeed returning home, just as Oedipus was returning home on all his journeyings. Perhaps the ultimate reduction of Tess, the distillation of her fate, is to be seen when she runs after Angel having murdered Alec. Angel turns round. "The tape-like surface of the road diminished in his rear as far as he could see, and as he gazed a moving spot intruded on the white vacuity of its perspective." This scene has been anticipated when Tess was working at Flintcomb-Ash: "the whole field was in colour a desolate drab; it was a complexion without features, as if a face, from chin to brow, should be only an expanse of skin. The sky wore, in another colour, the same likeness; a white vacuity of countenance with the lineaments gone. So these two upper and nether visages confronted each other all day long ... without anything standing between them but the two girls crawling over the surface of the former like flies." In both cases we see Tess as a moving spot on a white vacuity. And this extreme pictorial reduction seems to me to be right at the heart of Hardy's vision.

VI

To explain what I mean I want to interpose a few comments on some remarkable passages from the earlier novel, *Return of the Native*. Chapter One describes the vast inert heath. Chapter Two opens "Along the road walked an old man." He in turn sees a tiny speck of movement — "the single atom of life that the scene contained." And this spot is a "lurid red." It is, of course, the reddleman, but I want to emphasise the composition of the scene — the great stillness and the tiny spot of red movement which is the human presence on the heath. Shortly after, the reddleman is scanning the heath (Hardy's world is full of watching eyes) and it is then that he first sees Eustacia Vye. But how he first sees her is described in a passage which seems to me so central to Hardy that I want to quote at length.

There the form stood, motionless as the hill beneath. Above the plain rose the hill, above the hill rose the barrow, and above the barrow rose the figure. Above the figure there was nothing that could be mapped elsewhere than on a celestial globe.

Such a perfect, delicate, and necessary finish did the figure give to the dark pile of hills that it seemed to be the only obvious justification of their outline. Without it, there was the dome without the lantern; with it the architectural demands of the mass were satisfied. The scene was strangely homogeneous. The vale, the upland, the barrow, and the figure above it amounted to unity. Looking at this or that member of the group was not observing a complete thing, but a fraction of a thing.

The form was so much like an organic part of the entire motionless structure that to see it move would have impressed the mind as a strange phenomenon. Immobility being the chief characteristic of that whole which the person formed portion of, the discontinuance of immobility in any quarter suggested confusion.

Yet this is what happened. The figure perceptibly gave up its fixity, shifted a step or two, and turned round.

Here in powerful visual terms is a complete statement about existence. Without the human presence, sheer land and sky seem to have no formal, architectural significance. The human form brings significant outline to the brown mass of earth, the white vacuity of sky. But this moment of satisfying formal harmony depends on stillness, and to be human is to be animated, is to move. Hardy's novels are about "the discontinuance of immobility"; all the confusions that make up his plots are the result of people who perceptibly give up their fixity. To say that this is the very condition of life itself is only to point to the elemental nature of Hardy's art. All plants and all animals move, but much more within the rhythms ordained by their native terrain than humans — who build things like the *Titanic* and go plunging off into the night sea, or who set out in a horse and cart in the middle of the night to reach a distant market, in both cases meeting with disastrous accidents. Only what moves can crash. Eustacia moves on the still heath, breaking up the unity: there is confusion ahead for her. Not indeed that the heath is in a state of absolute fixity; that would imply a dead planet: "the quality of repose appertaining to the scene . . . was not the repose of actual stagnation, but the apparent repose of incredible slowness." Hardy often reminds us of the mindless insect life going on near the feet of his bewildered human protagonists; but to the human eye, which after all determines the felt meaning of the perceptible world, there is a move-

94

ment which is like stillness just as there is a motion which seems to be unmitigated violence. The "incredible slowness" of the heath, only serves to make more graphic the "catastrophic dash" which ends the lives of Eustacia and Wildeve. And after the "catastrophic dash" — "eternal rigidity."

The tragic tension between human and heath, between motion and repose, between the organic drive away from the inorganic and, what turns out to be the same thing, the drive to return to the inorganic, provides Hardy with the radical structure of his finest work. The human struggle against — and temporary departure from — the level stillness of the heath, is part of that struggle between the vertical and the horizontal which is a crucial part of Hardy's vision. We read of the "oppressive horizontality" of the heath, and when Eustacia comes to the time of her death Hardy describes her position in such a way that it echoes the first time we saw her, and completes the pattern of her life. She returns to one of those ancient earthen grave mounds, called barrows. "Eustacia at length reached Rainbarrow, and stood still there to think . . . she sighed bitterly and ceased to stand erect, gradually crouching down under the umbrella as if she were drawn into the Barrow by a hand from underneath." Her period of motion is over; her erect status above the flatness of the heath terminates at the same moment: she is, as it were, drawn back into the undifferentiated levelness of the earth from which she emerged. At the same time, you will remember, Susan is tormenting and burning a wax effigy of Eustacia, so that while she seems to be sinking back into the earth Hardy can also write "the effigy of Eustacia was melting to nothing." She is losing her distinguishing outline and features. Hardy describes elsewhere how a woman starts to "lose her own margin" when working in the fields. Human life is featured and contoured life; yet the erosion of feature and contour seems to be a primal activity of that "featureless convexity" of the heath, of the earth itself.

VII

This feeling of the constant attrition, and final obliteration, of the human shape and all human structures, permeates Hardy's work. Interviewed about Stonehenge he commented that "it is a matter of wonder that the erection has stood so long," adding however that "time nibbles year after year" at the structure. Just so he will write of a wind "which seemed to gnaw at the corners of the house"; of "wooden posts rubbed to a glossy smoothness by the flanks of infinite cows and calves of bygone years." His work is full of decaying architecture, and in *The Woodlanders* there is a memorable picture of the calves roaming in the ruins of Sherton Castle, "cooling their thirsty tongues by licking the quaint Norman carving, which glistened with the moisture." It is as though time, and all the rest of the natural order, conspired to eat away and erase all the structures and features associated with the human presence on, or intrusion into, the planet. Of one part of the heath Hardy says, in a sentence of extraordinarily succinct power, "There had been no obliteration, because there had been no tending." Tess working at Flintcomb-Ash in a landscape which is "a complexion without features," and Tess running after Angel, "a moving spot intruding on the white vacuity," is a visible paradigm of the terms of human life — a spot of featured animation moving painfully across a vast featureless repose. Like Eustacia, and like her wounded horse Prince, having remained upright as long as possible, she, too, simply "ceases to stand erect" and lies down on the flat sacrificial stone, as though offering herself not only up to the sun which tended her, but to the obliterating earth, the horizontal inertia of which she had disturbed.

Life is movement, and movement leads to confusion. Tess's instinct is for placidity, she recoils from rapid movements. Yet at crucial times she finds herself in men's carriages or men's machines. She has to drive her father's cart to market and Prince is killed. Alec forces her into his dog-cart which he drives recklessly at great speed. Of Tess we read "the least irregularity of motion startled her" and Alec at this point is disturbing and shaking up blood which will only be stilled in death. Angel, by contrast, takes Tess to the wedding in a carriage which manages to suggest something brutal, punitive, and funereal all at once — "It had stout wheelspokes, and heavy felloes, a great curved bed, immense straps and springs, and a pole like a battering-ram." All these man-made conveyances, together with the ominous train, and that "tyrant" the threshing machine, seem to threaten Tess. And yet she is bound to be involved in travelling, and dangerous motion, because she has no home. At the beginning the parson telling Tess's father about his noble lineage says an ominous thing. To Jack's question, " 'Where do we d'Urbervilles live?' " he answers: " 'You don't live anywhere. You are extinct — as a county family.' " Tess does not live anywhere. The one home she finds, Angel turns her out of. That is why she is bound to succumb to Alec. He provides a place but not a home. Alec takes her to Sandbourne, a place of "detached mansions," the very reverse of a community. It is a "pleasure city," "a glittering novelty," a place of meretricious fashion and amusement. " 'Tis all lodging-houses here. . . .' " This is the perfect place for the modern, deracinated Alec. It is no place at all for Tess, "a cottage girl." But we have seen her uprooted, forced to the roads, ejected from houses, knocking on doors which remain closed to her; we have seen the process by which she has become an exhausted helpless prey who is finally bundled off to a boarding house. Her spell in this place is a drugged interlude; she seems finally to have come to that state of catatonic trance which has been anticipated in previous episodes.

Angel realises that "Tess had spiritually ceased to recognize the body before him as hers — allowing it to drift, like a corpse upon the current, in a direction dissociated from its living will." Tess has been so "disturbed" by irregularities of motion, so pulled in different directions, that she really is sick, split, half dead. Hardy was very interested in this sort of split person — for instance, people with primitive instincts and modern nerves, as he says in another book — and we can see that Tess is subjected to too many different pressures, not to say torments, ever to achieve a felicitous wholeness of being.

VIII

This brings me to a problem I mentioned earlier. We see Tess suffering, apparently doomed to suffer; destroyed by two men, by society, by the sun outside her and the blood inside her. And we are tempted to ask, what is Hardy's vision of the *cause* of this tale of suffering. Throughout the book Hardy stresses that Tess is damned, and damns herself, according to man-made laws which are as arbitrary as they are cruel. He goes out of his way to show how Nature seems to disdain, ignore or make mockery of the laws which social beings impose on themselves. The fetish of chastity is a ludicrous aberration in a world which teems and spills with such promiscuous and far-flung fertility every year (not to say a brutal caricature of human justice in that what was damned in the woman was condoned in the man). So, if the book was an attempt to show an innocent girl who is destroyed by society though justified by Nature, Hardy could certainly have left the opposition as direct and as simple as that. Social laws hang Tess; and Nature admits no such laws. But it is an important part of the book that we feel Nature itself turning against Tess, so that we register something approaching a sadism of *both* the man-made *and* the natural directed against her. If she is tortured by the man-made threshing machine, she is also crushed by the forge of the sun; the cold negating metal in Angel is also to be found in the "steely stars"; the pangs of guilt which lacerate her are matched by the "glass splinters" of rain which penetrate her at Flintcomb-Ash. Perhaps to understand this feeling of almost universal opposition which grows throughout the book, we should turn to some of Hardy's own words, when he talks of "the universal harshness . . . the harshness of the position towards the temperament, of the means towards the aims, of today towards yesterday, or hereafter towards today." When he meditates on the imminent disappearance of the d'Urberville family he says, "so does Time ruthlessly destroy his own romances." This suggests a universe of radical opposition, working to destroy what it works to create, crushing to death what it coaxes into life. From this point of view society only appears as a functioning part of a larger process whereby the vertical returns to the horizontal, motion lapses into stillness and structure cedes to the unstructured. The policemen appear as the sun rises: Tess is a sacrifice to both, to all of them. Hardy's vision is tragic and penetrates far deeper than specific social anomalies. One is more inclined to think of Sophocles than, say, Zola, when reading Hardy. The vision is tragic because he shows an ordering of existence in which nature turns against itself, in which the sun blasts what it blesses, in which all the hopeful explorations of life turn out to have been a circuitous peregrination towards death. "All things are born to be diminished" said Pericles at the time of Sophocles; and Hardy's comparable feeling that all things are tended to be obliterated, reveals a Sophoclean grasp of the bed-rock ironies of existence.

Tess is the living demonstration of these tragic ironies. That is why she who is raped lives to be hanged; why she who is so physically beautiful feels guilt at "inhabiting the fleshly tabernacle with which Nature had endowed her"; why she who is a fertile source of life comes to feel that "birth itself was an ordeal of degrading personal compulsion, whose gratuitousness nothing in the result seemed to justify." It is why she attracts the incompatible forces represented by Alec and Angel. It is why she who is a lover is also a killer. Tess is gradually crucified on the oppugnant ironies of circumstance and existence itself, ironies which centre, I have suggested, on the fact of blood, that basic stuff which starts the human spot moving across the white vacuity. Blood, and the spilling of blood; which in one set of circumstances can mean sexual passion and the creation of life, and in another can mean murderous passion and death — two forms of "red" energy intimately related — this is the substance of Tess's story. And why should it all happen to her? You can say, as some people in the book say fatalistically, " 'It was to be.' " Or you could go through the book and try to work out how Hardy apportions the blame — a bit on Tess, a bit on society, a bit on religion, a bit on heredity, a bit on the Industrial Revolution, a bit on the men who abuse her, a bit on the sun and the stars, and so on. But Hardy does not work in this way. More than make us judge, Hardy makes us see; and in looking for some explanation of why all this should happen to Tess, our eyes finally settle on that red ribbon marking out the little girl in the white dress, which already foreshadows the red blood stain on the white ceiling. In her beginning is her end. It is the oldest of truths, but it takes a great writer to make us experience it again in all its awesome mystery.

IX

Hardy specifically rejected the idea of offering any theory of the universe. In his General Preface to his works, he said "Nor is it likely, indeed, that imaginative writings extending over more than forty years would exhibit a coherent scientific theory of the universe even if it had been attempted — of the universe concerning which Spencer owns to the 'paralyzing thought' that possibly there exists no comprehension of it anywhere. But such objectless consistency never has been attempted. . . ." Hardy "theorizes" far less than Lawrence, but certain images recur which serve to convey his sense of life — its poignancy and its incomprehensibility — more memorably than any overt statement. Death, the sudden end of brilliance and movement, occupied a constant place in his thoughts. "The most prosaic man becomes a poem when you stand by his grave and think of him" he once wrote; and the strange brightness of ephemeral creatures is something one often meets in his fiction — pictorially, not philosophically. "Gnats, knowing nothing of their brief glorification, wandered across the shimmer of this pathway, irradiated as if they bore fire within them, then passed out of its line, and were quite extinct." Compare with that the description of the girls returning from the dance: "and as they went there moved onward with them . . . a circle of opalized light, formed by the moon's rays upon the glistening sheet of dew. Each pedestrian could see no halo but his or her own. . . ." Hardy is often to be found stressing the ephemeral nature of life — "independent worlds of ephemerons were passing their time in mad carousal," "ephemeral creatures, took up their positions where only a year ago others had stood in their place when these were nothing more than germs and inorganic particles" — and it often seems that the ephemeral fragments of moving life are also like bubbles of light, temporary illuminations of an encroaching darkness. One of the great scenes in all of Hardy is in *The Return of the Native* when Wildeve and Venn, the reddleman, gamble at night on the heath. Their lantern makes a little circle of light which draws things out of the darkness towards it. "The light of the candle had by this time attracted heath-flies, moths and other winged creatures of night, which floated round the lantern, flew into the flame, or beat about the faces of the two players." Much more suggestively as they continue to throw dice; "they were surrounded by dusky forms about four feet high, standing a few paces beyond the rays of the lantern. A moment's inspection revealed that the encircling figures were heath-croppers, their heads being all towards the players, at whom they gazed intently." When a moth extinguishes the candle, Wildeve gathers glow worms and puts them on the stone on which they are playing. "The incongruity between the men's deeds and their environment was great. Amid the soft juicy vegetation of the hollow in which they sat, the motionless and the uninhabited solitude, intruded the chink of guineas, the rattle of dice, the exclamations of the reckless players." Again, it is one of those scenes which seems to condense a whole vision of human existence — a strange activity in a small circle of light, and all round them the horses of the night noiselessly gathering at the very perimeter. And in *Tess of the d'Urbervilles* Hardy develops this scene into a metaphor of great power. He is describing how Tess's love for Angel sustains her: "it enveloped her as a photosphere, irradiated her into forgetfulness of her past sorrows, keeping back the gloomy spectres that would persist in their attempts to touch her — doubt, fear, moodiness, care, shame. She knew that they were waiting like wolves just outside the circumscribing light, but she had long spells of power to keep them in hungry subjection there. . . . She walked in brightness, but she knew that in the background those shapes of darkness were always spread."

I have singled out this image not only because I think there is something quintessentially Hardyan in it, but also because I think it is an image which profoundly influenced D. H. Lawrence.

Selected Criticisms

Mr. Hardy has written a novel that is not only good, but great. Tess herself stands, a credible, sympathetic creature in the very forefront of his women. . . .

. . . But was it needful that Mr. Hardy should challenge criticism upon what is after all a side issue? His business was rather to fashion (as he has done) a being of flesh and blood than to propose the suffering woman's view of a controversy which only the dabbler in sexual ethics can enjoy. Why should a novelist embroil himself in moral technicalities? As it is, one half suspects Mr. Hardy of a desire to argue out the justice of the comparative punishments meted to man and to woman for sexual aberrations. To have fashioned a faultless piece of art built upon the great tragic model were surely sufficient. And, as a matter of fact, the "argumentation" is confined to the preface and sub-title, which are, to our thinking, needless and a diversion from the main interest, which lies not in Tess, the sinner or sinned against, but in Tess the woman. Mr. Hardy's style is here, as always, suave and supple, although his use of scientific and ecclesiastical terminology grows excessive. Nor is it quite befitting that a novelist should sneer at a character with the word "antinomianism," and employ "determinism" for his own purposes a page or two later. And a writer who aims so evidently at impartiality had been well advised in restraining a slight animosity (subtly expressed though it be) against certain conventions which some people even yet respect. However, all things taken into account, 'Tess of the D'Urbervilles' is well in front of Mr. Hardy's previous work, and is destined, there can be no doubt, to rank high among the achievements of Victorian novelists.

The Athenaeum, January 9, 1892.

Mr. Hardy's latest novel is his greatest. Amid his beloved Wessex valleys and uplands and among the unsophisticated folk in whose lives and labours we have learned from him to find unsuspected dignity and romance, he has founded a story, daring in its treatment of conventional ideas, pathetic in its sadness, and profoundly stirring in its tragic power . . . It is well that an idealist like Mr. Hardy should remind us how terribly defective are our means of judging others.

The London *Times*, January 13, 1892.

Let it at once be said that there is not one single touch of nature either in John Durbeyfield or in any other character in the book. All are stagey, and some are farcical. Tess herself comes the nearest to possibility, and is an attractive figure; but even she is suggestive of the carefully-studied simplicity of the theatre, and not at all of the carelessness of the fields . . . The story gains nothing by the reader being let into the secret of the physical attributes which especially fascinated [Alec D'Urberville] in Tess. Most people can fill in blanks for themselves, without its being necessary to put the dots on the i's so very plainly; but Mr. Hardy leaves little unsaid. "She had an attribute which amounted to a disadvantage just now; and it was this that caused Alec D'Urberville's eyes to rivet themselves upon her. It was a luxuriance of aspect; a fulness of growth, which made her appear more of a woman than she really was. She had inherited the feature from her mother without the quality it denoted." It is these side suggestions that render Mr. Hardy's story so very disagreeable, and *Tess* is full of them . . . It matters much less what a story is about than how that story is told, and Mr. Hardy, it must be conceded, tells an unpleasant story in a very unpleasant way. He says that it "represents, on the whole, a true sequence of events"; but does it? The impression of most readers will be that Tess, never having cared for D'Urberville even in her early days, hating him as the cause of her ruin, and, more so, as the cause of her separation from Clare, whom she madly loved, would have died by the roadside sooner than go back and live with him and be decked out with fine clothes. Still, Mr. Hardy did well to let her pay the full penalty, and not die among the monoliths of Stonehenge, as many writers would have done.

The Saturday Review, January 16, 1892.

Hardy's true greatness, if it is to be found in his fiction, cannot be said to reside in his short stories, memorable as they often are, but must be sought in his novels, more particularly his later novels. . . . All these work towards a sombre dénouement and must be regarded as the practical application of Hardy's lifelong notemaking on the subject of 'tragedy.' . . . *Tess* is the most poignant of all Hardy's stories. This is not because of anything that the heroine may be thought to symbolize, or any thesis that may be implied, but because Hardy is here writing more singly than in any other work about casual wrong, the will to recover, the growth of love, faithfulness, frail happiness, and death. It is a much simpler novel than most of Hardy's, and it contains some of his best writing as well as some of his worst.

G. D. Klingopulos, in *The Pelican Guide to English Literature: From Dickens to Hardy*, 1958.

Hardy was praised or blamed by some of his contemporaries for austerity and subtlety, and for a seeming evasion of popular modes. But the Conrads and Joyces and Prousts and Kafkas have intervened to change our view of both the novel and the world. Today Hardy would appear to survive rather as a popular and even primitive novelist, reaching us through pure narrative gifts and antique simplicities of understanding and art. . . . The love of the macabre coincidence and grotesque mischance, the cruel imaginings and manipulations, all the bad luck and all the mismatched destinies, the darkness of the physical and moral landscapes, the awareness of dwindling energies, and the sense of man's appalling limitations — these are peculiarly modern. Yet quite as fundamental are a timeless traditionalism and an unmodern purity of temperament and a most uninhibited compassion. For behind Hardy's sadistic imaginings and pessimistic declarations lie, of course, a deep concern for the fortunes of his characters, an incorrigible sympathy for all who are lonely and all who long for happiness. Man usually deserved, Hardy believed, more than he received.

Albert Guerard, *Hardy: A Collection of Critical Essays*, 1963.

The greatest element of appeal in *Tess* is the pathos inherent in the story. . . . It is this pathos — voicing itself in accents of great beauty — that marks the superiority of *Tess* to any other English novel of this period.

Joseph Warren Beach, *The Technique of Thomas Hardy*, 1922.

The major nineteenth-century novelist was a figure of common sense, redirecting the vulgar and the eccentric into acceptable behavior and burlesquing them if they remained obtuse and selfish. By the time of George Eliot and Thomas Hardy, however, laughter is insufficient in a world in which the innocent as well as the guilty can be destroyed not through their own foibles but through life itself. Hardy's bleak outlook becomes the norm: the novelist no longer suggested darkness in a world of light, but now occasioned light in a world of darkness, and frequently the light revealed the path to self-destruction.

Frederick R. Karl, *A Reader's Guide to The Nineteenth-Century British Novel*, 1964.

Undoubtedly, it would seem, the long years of personal unhappiness intensified his mood of revolt against a Power indifferent to man's misfortunes. He had always been inclined to collect instances of futile tragedy but the disposition grew so that the situations which Hardy devised for his characters seem often deliberately cruel as in *Tess* and deliberately squalid as in *Jude the Obscure*. He became an ingenious inventor of Life's Little Ironies. It was justifiably said by a reviewer of one of his last published collections of stories: "He just decoys his characters one by one into a circumstantial *cul de sac* and steadily blocks the entry."

One may be conscious of the weakness of Hardy's work and at the same time feel its greatness profoundly. His anger with God for not being there, as someone once described Hardy's attitude, has the effect of making his greatest figures, Eustacia and Clym in *The Return of the*

Native, Henchard in *The Mayor of Casterbridge* and Tess, extraordinarily impressive, while his descriptions of nature and of country life are Victor Hugoesque in quality. There is the same deep poetic feeling for Nature as a whole in Hardy as in Victor Hugo, the same fine observation of detail. The massive reality and Biblical beauty of Hardy's pictures of rural occupations have surely never been surpassed. The vigil of the shepherd in lambing time, the sheep fair, the thunderstorm breaking up the fine harvest weather, the inside of the malthouse and its gossip, are scenes which Shakespeare or even Chaucer might have watched and Shakespeare himself might have created their attendant rustics.

Hardy wrote only one novel which profoundly stirred his readers to sympathy, *Tess of the D'Urbervilles*. He did not reach their emotions in his other books, though from the publication of *The Return of the Native*, in 1878, he had been regarded as in the forefront of British novelists. His designation of Tess as "a pure woman" roused enormous criticism, but mainly from people such as the mistress who found her maid reading it open at the chapter headed "Maiden No More" and confiscated the book. *Jude* was said to have been burnt by a Bishop, which amused Hardy, though other sounder criticism touched him so on the raw that he wrote no more novels and turned again to poetry.

Irene Cooper Willis, NSN. June 1, 1940.

Hardy takes a short cut to tragedy by reducing life to a formula. He gets rid beforehand of the main obstacle to tragedy, which is man's natural inclination to avoid it. His characters are passive, or at the best endlessly patient. He does not believe that character is fate; so that for him tragedy does not proceed from action, but resides with the power which determines all action. Misfortune is not brought about by men and women, but is arranged by this power which is indifferent to all arrangements and therefore to misfortune itself. Misfortune is a principle of the universe and falls upon the weak and the strong indiscriminately, neither averted by wisdom nor brought on by folly, striking inevitably and yet as if by chance. For it is the result of a mistake which man cannot correct, since he did not make it. It was made by the Maker of the universe. . . .

Hardy was partial to man; to be partial is to be involuntarily unjust; and in taking evil from man's shoulders he robbed man of one of his indispensable possessions. For in relieving man of evil he did not improve his situation, but made it worse, since he concentrated all evil against him. His characters, therefore, are curiously neutral; they gain colour only when passion or misfortune touches them, and are quite convincing only in their helplessness and instability. He draws women better than men. He sees woman and her response to love almost with a woman's eyes. He is on woman's side against man, just as he is on man's side against nature, and for the same reason; for woman is the final victim. He drew one man of strong and active character, Michael Henchard in *The Mayor of Casterbridge*. But most of his men are simple or priggish or effeminate. Their highest virtue is uncomplaining endurance of misfortune, a virtue which they share with women. In describing endurance Hardy is best, for by enduring man seems to rise above the malice of fate by a pure act of magnanimity comprehensible only to himself. The peasants who form a chorus to the novels are the final expression of this endurance, which has become so native to them that it has been transformed into a kind of humour. They are too low to fear a fall. They are in the position where the universe wants to have them; therefore beyond the reach of tragedy: the speakers of the epilogue to every action.

Edwin Muir, Essays on Literature and Society (Hogarth Pr., 1949).

In his lifetime, Thomas Hardy, though widely admired, had to suffer a good deal of abuse from critics whom he himself described as "manipulators . . . professed literary boxers who put on their convictions for the occasion." Yet these, in the long run, have been less damaging to him than that other minority which, professing urbanity, assumed that it could safely patronize him. "A little man with an earthy face," "clumsy," "autodidact": these and similar phrases have set the tone. George Eliot and Lawrence have also been called "autodidacts," which I think must be the critical equivalent of "peasant," since George Eliot was one of the best-educated women of her time, and both Hardy and Lawrence had quite good formal educations. The distinction really being offered is one of class, in its modern critical disguise of small urbanity. Hardy's open and strong feelings, in combination with his attachment to ordinarily inarticulate people, have continually exposed him to the worst that crude sophistication can manage. The defense is only just beginning to get established. . . .

Hardy wrote, not like one man, but like at least three, and the question of how good a writer he is cannot be settled by ordinary norms, but only by analysis of this fragmentation. There is a similar though much smaller division in George Eliot, and the case of whether Lawrence wrote well (it is common observation that he wrote both magnificently and very badly) is also relevant. With Hardy, the analysis is simpler than with either George Eliot or Lawrence: the fragmentation is much more on the surface, and the language of powerful description and dialogue, the language of firm statement, and the language of pretension and accommodation to fashionable academic and literary styles can be picked up almost as separate layers. The complexity of his social history as a writer can then be related to these variations.

Raymond Williams, MGW, May 4, 1961.

Suggested Study Topics

In order to achieve a more enlightened and comprehensive view and evaluation of *Tess of the d'Urbervilles* the following study topics and/or assignments are suggested for the reader's use.

1. Symbolism and allusion have a considerable place in *Tess*. Discuss the significance of the following:

   a. the incident of the dead pheasants.
   b. the killing of the snakes and rodents at the bottom of the stack.
   c. the capture at Stonehenge.
   d. the dairy farm.
   e. Tess in the stone coffin in the "ruined choir."
   f. the sleepwalking.
   g. the darkness of the forest where the seduction takes place.
   h. the blind woman and her chickens.
   i. the paintings of the ancient d'Urberville women.
   j. the gift of blood pudding and mead.
   k. Angel's carrying of the girls across the swollen river.
   l. the steam harvester.
   m. the crowing of the afternoon cock.
   n. the migration to Brazil, a Catholic country.
   o. the names of Angel Clare, and Mercy Chant.

2. Following are two of Aristotle's requisites for tragedy:
   Tragedy must involve "the character of a person neither eminently virtuous or just, nor yet involved in misfortune by deliberate vice or villainy, but by some error of human frailty"; and, "tragedy is an imitation of some action that is serious, entire and of some magnitude, . . . effecting through pity and terror the refinement of these passions." Discuss *Tess* as conforming to or departing from these criteria.

3. Hardy is much concerned with irony, a word for which he sometimes seems to have a personal, private definition. One of his novels is called *Life's Little Ironies*. In Chapter 53, we find, " 'O, it is not Angel — not my son — the Angel who went away!' she cried in all the irony of sorrow, as she turned herself aside." In Chapter 45, Tess is "quite sick with the irony of the contrast." Five other uses of this word appear in the book. Try to establish whether Hardy was systematic and consistent in his use of the word; what his use of it actually connotes; and what part it plays in the book.

4. Discuss the various approaches to religion shown in *Tess*.

5. Applications of Questions 3 and 4 above are shown in the following two quotations: 1. (Chapter 53) "Their Christianity was such that, reprobates being their especial care, the tenderness toward Tess which her blood, her simplicity, even her poverty, had not engendered, was instantly excited by her sin;" 2. (Chapter 15) "Though to visit the sins of the fathers upon the children may be a morality good enough for divinities, it is scorned by average human nature." Discuss Hardy's own attitude toward conventional religion as shown in these two quotations.

6. Two parts of the book have been much ridiculed by critics: the sleep-walking of Angel, and the sighing, passionate love of four dairymaids for one man. Is this criticism valid or invalid?

7. Describe the influence of nature or natural environment upon Tess in the various sections of the tale.

8. What part does each of the following play in Tess' tragedy: (a) her parents, (b) Alec, (c) Angel?

9. What effect does the knowledge of the d'Urberville heritage have on: (a) Tess' parents, (b) Tess, (c) Angel?

10. How does Tess' life exemplify "the inherent will to enjoy and the circumstantial forces against enjoyment?"

11. Choose a scene in the novel which you consider especially noteworthy, and show how the author has presented it effectively.

12. Describe the effect of the setting on the action of the novel. Give examples.

13. Discuss the manifestations of Fate as they affect the life of Tess.

14. From your experience, which of these characters do you find more true to life: (a) Angel, (b) Alec, (c) Angel's father?

15. How would the story be different if: (a) Angel had danced with Tess when he first saw her, (b) Tess' letter had been received by Angel, (c) Tess had visited the Clares?

16. In what ways does Tess contribute to her own tragedy? Discuss.

17. Compare and contrast the characters of Alec and Angel.

Bibliography

Abercrombie, Lascelles. *Thomas Hardy, A Critical Study*. New York: Russell & Russell, 1965.

Beach, Joseph Warren. *The Technique of Thomas Hardy*. New York: Russell & Russell, 1962.

Blunden, Edmund. *Thomas Hardy*. New York: St. Martin's Press, 1962.

Carpenter, Richard C. *Thomas Hardy*. New York: Twayne Publishers, Inc., 1964.

Cecil, Lord David. *Hardy the Novelist*. London: Constable & Co., Ltd., 1943.

Chase, Mary Ellen. *Thomas Hardy: From Serial to Novel*. New York: Russell & Russell, 1964.

Chew, Samuel C. *Thomas Hardy, Poet and Novelist*. New York: Alfred A. Knopf, 1929.

Duffin, Henry C. *Thomas Hardy: A Study of the Wessex Novels*. 3rd ed. New York: Barnes & Noble, 1962.

Firor, Ruth A. *Folkways in Thomas Hardy*. New York: A. S. Barnes, 1962.

Ford, Boris (ed.). *The Pelican Guide to English Literature: From Dickens to Hardy*. Baltimore: Penguin Books, 1958.

Grimsditch, Herbert B. *Character and Environment in the Novels of Thomas Hardy*. London: H.F. & G. Witherby, 1925.

Guerard, Albert J. *Hardy: A Collection of Critical Essays*. Englewood Cliffs, N.J.: Prentice-Hall, Inc., 1963.

Hardy, Evelyn. *Thomas Hardy, A Critical Biography*. London: 1954.

Howe, Irving. *Thomas Hardy* ("Masters of World Literature" Series). New York: MacMillan, 1968.

Hawkins, Desmond. *Thomas Hardy*. London: A. Barker, 1950.

Karl, F. R. *A Reader's Guide to the Nineteenth-Century British Novel*. New York: Farrar, Straus & Giroux (Noonday Press Edition), 1964.

Mickelson, Anne Z. *Thomas Hardy's Women and Men: The Defeat of Nature*. Metuchen, N.J.: Scarecrow Press, 1976.

Scott-James, R. A. *Thomas Hardy*. London: Longmans, Green, 1951.

Watt, Ian (ed.). *The Victorian Novel*. London: Oxford University Press, 1971.

Wing, George. *Thomas Hardy*. Edinburgh: Oliver & Boyd Ltd., 1963.